Making Grades Matter

Standards-Based Grading in a Secondary PLC at Work®

MATT TOWNSLEY   NATHAN L. WEAR

Solution Tree | Press

a division of
Solution Tree

555 North Morton Street
Bloomington, IN 47404
800.733.6786 (toll free) / 812.336.7700
FAX: 812.336.7790

email: info@SolutionTree.com
SolutionTree.com

Visit **go.SolutionTree.com/PLCbooks** to download the free reproducibles in this book.

Printed in the United States of America

Library of Congress Cataloging-in-Publication Data

Names: Townsley, Matt, author. | Wear, Nathan L., author.
Title: Making grades matter : standards-based grading in a secondary PLC at
   work / Matt Townsley, Nathan L. Wear.
Description: Bloomington, IN : Solution Tree Press, [2020] | Includes
   bibliographical references and index.
Identifiers: LCCN 2019041127 (print) | LCCN 2019041128 (ebook) | ISBN
   9781949539653 (paperback) | ISBN 9781949539660 (ebook)
Subjects: LCSH: Grading and marking (Students) | Professional learning
   communities. | Education, Secondary. | Educational evaluation. |
   Educational tests and measurements.
Classification: LCC LB3051 .T65 2020 (print) | LCC LB3051 (ebook) | DDC
   371.27/2--dc23
LC record available at https://lccn.loc.gov/2019041127
LC ebook record available at https://lccn.loc.gov/2019041128

Solution Tree
Jeffrey C. Jones, CEO
Edmund M. Ackerman, President

Solution Tree Press
President and Publisher: Douglas M. Rife
Associate Publisher: Sarah Payne-Mills
Art Director: Rian Anderson
Managing Production Editor: Kendra Slayton
Senior Production Editor: Todd Brakke
Content Development Specialist: Amy Rubenstein
Copy Editor: Jessi Finn
Proofreader: Elisabeth Abrams
Text and Cover Designer: Laura Cox
Editorial Assistant: Sarah Ludwig

Acknowledgments

We would like to thank the educators around the United States who are doing this important work around standards-based grading. We are especially indebted to the teachers at the Solon Community School District (Solon, Iowa) who spent years implementing these grading principles. You are the inspiration for this book! We are also indebted to Dr. Cathy Vatterott who first encouraged us to put our ideas down on paper. We also thank the editorial board at Solution Tree for taking a chance on us first-time authors eager to share our standards-based grading successes and struggles so that others may benefit.

Acknowledgments from Matt Townsley:

I would like to acknowledge the persistence of my coauthor, Nathan. After many phone calls, starts and stops, and countless evening hours writing down our ideas, thank you for sticking with this project—we did it! I would also like to express a deep appreciation for the educators in my family, Eric and Russ, in particular, for their willingness to engage in discussions centered on grading and assessment during our holiday meals together. Thank you, too, to the rest of the Townsley family, who willingly listened as we monopolized Christmas, Thanksgiving, and birthday conversations for far too many hours! No project could be complete without the unwavering support of my bride and best friend, Cassy. Finally, I would like to acknowledge my parents, Mike and Diane Townsley. No matter the outcome or circumstances in life, you have reminded me to "count everything as loss because of the surpassing worth of knowing Christ Jesus my Lord" (Philippians 3:8a).

Acknowledgments from Nathan L. Wear:

I would first and foremost like to thank my family. To my wife, Anne, and my kids, Rhyse and Lauryn, you mean the world to me. My parents, Larry and Susan, your love and appreciation are beyond measure. The family dinner conversations around schools, leadership, and education have helped craft who I am as an educational leader.

Professionally, I have worked with many great people. All of you, in some way, have contributed to my belief in schools, and I am forever thankful. To the staff at Solon High School, I dedicate this work to you. Your tireless devotion to educational excellence is present in all the work you do. I have never in my career been surrounded by a greater group of people. We always said we wanted to be state champs in the classroom. This book highlights our success.

To my awesome administrative colleagues, Sam Miller, Jodi Rickels, and Mike Herdliska, our commitment to being better together motivates me every day. To my coauthor, Matt Townsley, who encouraged me to put words to paper, I thank you for your incredible leadership and friendship. Those car rides to Minnesota were never lacking in fruitful conversation or thought. Finally, I want to thank my grandmother, Ruth Schwiebert, who was a career elementary teacher. Her love of reading was contagious, and she always had a book for me or a quick recommendation for a good read. Now, it's my time to return the favor.

Solution Tree Press would like to thank the following reviewers:

JoDee Adney
High School Special Education and History Teacher
Clinton High School
Clinton, Oklahoma

Kim Ballestro
Assistant Principal
Carterville Intermediate School
Carterville Junior High School
Carterville, Illinois

Adam Dyche
Social Studies Department Chair
Waubonsie Valley High School
Aurora, Illinois

Kelly Hilliard
Mathematics Teacher
McQueen High School
Reno, Nevada

Andrew Kozlowsky
Social Studies Teacher
Quince Orchard High School
Gaithersburg, Maryland

Paula Maeker
Solution Tree Associate
Spring, Texas

Matthew Robinson
Mathematics Teacher
Edmond Memorial High School
Edmond, Oklahoma

Scott Sullivan
Director of Curriculum, Instruction, and Assessment
Estacada School District
Estacada, Oregon

Table of Contents

Reproducible pages are in italics.

About the Authors

Matt Townsley, EdD, is an assistant professor of educational leadership at the University of Northern Iowa in Cedar Falls, Iowa. He is a former district administrator and teacher in Solon Community School District, also in Iowa, where he led curriculum, assessment, and school-improvement initiatives, all with a professional learning community culture as the foundation. *District Administration* magazine named Solon Community Schools a district of distinction in 2015, and Solution Tree recognized multiple buildings in the district as model professional learning communities during his tenure. Through conferences, professional development, and workshops, Matt has consulted with thousands of teachers and administrators across the United States on the topics of assessment and standards-based grading.

In 2017, Matt was named Iowa's Central Office Administrator of the Year, and in 2014, he was recognized as an Association for Supervision and Curriculum Development Emerging Leader. His writing has been published in journals such as *Educational Leadership, School Administrator, NASSP Bulletin, The Journal of School Administration Research and Development*, and *American Secondary Education*.

Matt received a bachelor's degree in mathematics education from Wartburg College, a master's degree in curriculum and instructional technology from Iowa State University, a certificate of advanced study in educational leadership from the University of Northern Iowa, and a doctorate in school improvement from the University of West Georgia.

To learn more about Matt's work, visit www.mctownsley.net or follow @mctownsley on Twitter.

Nathan L. Wear is associate superintendent and chief academic officer of Linn-Mar Community School District in Marion, Iowa, a district of nearly eight thousand students. He also serves as an adjunct professor at Viterbo University in La Crosse, Wisconsin. He is the former principal of Solon High School in Solon, Iowa, where he and his staff championed grading reform efforts and implemented standards-based grading within a professional learning community. During his time in Solon, his staff were recognized as a model professional learning community, and *U.S. News and World Report* named Solon High School one of the best U.S. high schools in 2014. Prior to Solon, Nathan was the principal of Pence Elementary in Fairfield, Iowa. He has been an educator since 2002, with a background in elementary teaching, standards-based grading, and assessment.

Nathan is an active member of the School Administrators of Iowa, a statewide organization committed to providing support and development for Iowa's school leaders. His strong belief in leading with a positive organizational culture through high accountability has resulted in a marked improvement in the schools where he has worked. Nathan has presented throughout Iowa and Minnesota to principals, teachers, superintendents, and other school leaders on topics ranging from standards-based grading to professional learning communities, and he has provided school leaders with valuable professional development in those areas.

Nathan received his bachelor's degree in elementary education from Wartburg College and a master's degree in educational administration from Texas State University. He received his superintendent endorsement from the University of Northern Iowa and is currently finishing his doctorate in educational leadership at the same institution.

To learn more about Nathan's work, visit https://nathanwear.wixsite.com/leadership and follow @Nathan_Wear on Twitter.

To book Matt Townsley or Nathan L. Wear for professional development, contact pd@SolutionTree.com.

Introduction

By Nathan L. Wear

I'll never forget the day in September of 2011 when several students showed up in my office demanding to be moved to another section of class with a different teacher. I was serving as principal at Solon High School in Solon, Iowa, and we were in the initial stages of investigating practices of standards-based grading. However, our implementation was inconsistent, and we had yet to develop any schoolwide principles. Understandably, this frustrated many of our students. In the case of these students, one section's teacher was allowing retakes and reassessments, and the other was not. One teacher was counting homework in the final grade, while the other was not. Both teachers were masterful instructors, teaching the same course and content, yet they had set up their grading practices in completely different ways. I thought to myself, "Is this fair for students?"

Recognizing this issue and the challenge this situation presented, I picked up the phone and called my colleague Matt Townsley, coauthor of this book and director of instruction in the Solon Community School District at the time. The conversation that followed was the spark that ignited a multiyear journey to successfully implement standards-based grading in a rural Iowa school district. Ultimately, it was a journey well worth taking, but it's a challenging undertaking, and we believe this resource can help schools and districts meet this challenge.

Put simply, Matt and I define *standards-based grading* as a philosophy of learning and assessment that centers on three core principles.

1. Grades should communicate students' current levels of learning based on standards.

2. Homework should serve as ungraded practice.

3. Students should have multiple opportunities to demonstrate their learning.

Although these principles are common at elementary levels, which already often operate in a standards-based manner through the use of report cards organized by standard, they are also very important for secondary schools; however, they are more challenging to implement at the secondary level because these schools must incorporate standards-based grading practices with more traditional norms, including letter grades, class rank, activities eligibility, honor rolls, and other ranking or sorting norms.

Overhauling grading practices at Solon High School to align with these principles would shift both our school and district away from the traditional reporting of grades for homework, projects, and tests.

At the time, we had individual teachers dabbling in these standards-based grading principles, but we hadn't collectively defined them. Fortunately, there was a desire among staff to rethink how our secondary schools graded students. Intensifying this desire was our collaborative work with the professional learning community (PLC) process, in which we had established grade-level, disciplinary, and vertical teams throughout the district to pursue the three big ideas of a PLC: (1) a focus on learning rather than teaching, (2) a collaborative culture, and (3) a results orientation in which collecting evidence of learning is essential (DuFour, DuFour, Eaker, Many, & Mattos, 2016). Further, achieving these aims meant addressing the four critical questions of a PLC (DuFour et al., 2016):

1. What knowledge, skills, and dispositions should every student acquire as a result of this unit, this course, or this grade level?
2. How will we know when each student has acquired the essential knowledge and skills?
3. How will we respond when some students do not learn?
4. How will we extend the learning for students who are already proficient? (p. 36)

When our district started to dig into these four critical questions, we knew we couldn't answer them through our traditional grading practices at the secondary level. Thankfully, our elementary building already had a standards-based report card in place from which we could build.

As our phone discussion continued, Matt and I realized implementing this grading change at the secondary schools was going to be a challenge. After all, secondary schools have a long-standing tradition of points-based gradebooks, percentages, and letter grades. We set out to change our practice by implementing standards-based grading within our school's PLC process. Over six years, we were able to improve student achievement at our already high-achieving buildings. Prior to our journey, 85 percent of our students were proficient, and 25 percent of our students were highly proficient in nearly all grade levels and content areas on the state standardized test. By the end of our journey, nearly 90 percent of our students were proficient, and nearly 30 percent of our students were highly proficient in reading, mathematics, science, and social studies. Our ACT scores also continued to improve, outpacing the state average.

Although we are proud of these successes, we should note that our greatest achievement was not improved standardized test scores but the sheer number of students increasing success through their coursework. Before our implementation of standards-based grading, on average, 10 percent of our students would fail a course. After implementation, that number dropped to less than 3 percent. This strikes to the heart of the PLC philosophy, ensuring that *all* students succeed. Through this book, we hope to help secondary-level teachers and administrators working in a PLC to successfully adopt standards-based grading at their school or district.

What This Book Is About

We designed this book to assist readers in explicitly connecting the concepts of standards-based grading with the principles of PLCs as Richard DuFour, Rebecca DuFour, Robert Eaker, Thomaas W. Many, and Mike Mattos (2016) envision them in *Learning by Doing.* Several other authors are also contributing to the literature on the need to reform grading practices. You may be familiar with the writings of Thomas R. Guskey (2015a), Tammy Heflebower (Heflebower, Hoegh, & Warrick, 2014), Robert J. Marzano (2010), Ken O'Connor (2018), Douglas Reeves (2016), Rick Wormeli (2011), and others, all of whom you will find listed in the references and resources section of this book. Many of their books are written with K–12 audiences in mind and aim to convince readers of the need to change grading practices. These are important and valuable works; however, we feel grades 6–12 educators have an unmet need for a book that explains in grounded terms how they can make this change work in practice. Our goal is to provide a practical how-to book for the thousands of secondary-level educators working in a PLC that makes explicit connections between the work of a PLC and the implementation of standards-based grading in secondary schools. As authors and educators, we believe that secondary schools cannot accomplish standards-based grading practices without a strong foundation in the PLC process.

Who This Book Is For

Despite standards-based grading's growing popularity in elementary schools (Iamarino, 2014), transitioning it to secondary schools continues to evoke emotion and dissent in some communities (Frankin, Buckmiller, & Kruse, 2016). This is because standards-based grading practices have not always been part of education at this level, and it is not always clear how these practices align with many colleges' and universities' long-held admissions standards. In one school district, the board of education voted against expanding standards-based grading practices across its high school due to a perception it would affect "students' higher education opportunities, especially concerning how important grade point averages and scholarships are to college and university admissions, as well as honor rolls" (Holland, 2018). We know this is not an isolated case. As such, we wrote this book for secondary teachers and administrators who recognize the need to shift secondary grading practices but who lack the tools, clarity, and buy-in for making the change.

Some of you reading this may have some working knowledge of standards-based grading principles and PLCs but have not yet connected these practices or implemented the changes you desire in your setting. You will benefit from this book's practical steps, pitfalls to avoid, and guidance on how to align standards-based grading with the four critical questions of a PLC. When you start your grading reform journey, we recommend first reading one of the many books from authors we listed in What This Book Is About (page 3) that describe *why* grading practices need to change. After all, strong leadership teams rely on the perspectives of many respected educators. We believe our book provides an excellent practical link to such great authors' and practitioners' theories by explaining *how* to implement standards-based grading at the secondary level within a PLC.

How This Book Is Organized

Because the purpose of this book is to provide a road map that will help secondary school PLCs implement standards-based grading, we structured it to clarify the practices necessary to implement this change and examine how standards-based grading aligns with the big ideas of a PLC.

We based the chapters in this book on the three standards-based grading principles we established at the start of this introduction. Chapter 1 elaborates on the three principles that we believe best define standards-based grading and how standards-based grading aligns to the big ideas and critical questions of a PLC. Chapters 2, 3, and 4 each delve into one of the three principles of standards-based grading and provide the tools necessary to implement standards-based grading within a PLC. Specifically, chapter 2 gives guidance for communicating current levels of learning based on standards, chapter 3 shows how teams and schools can implement homework as ungraded practice, and chapter 4 details how teachers can offer students multiple opportunities to demonstrate their understanding of a learning standard. While we focus specifically on teacher teams in these chapters, administrators and leadership teams reading these chapters will be able to identify ways they can better support their PLC. Finally, chapter 5 provides practical steps for implementation teams consisting of secondary administrators, curriculum leaders, teachers, and others who are leading the process for implementing standards-based grading in a PLC.

Chapters 2–5 each include standards-based grading continua to help you assess your current level of understanding and implementation of either the chapter's defining principle or the high-level administrative work of implementing standards-based grading. Each also includes an action-plan template you can use individually and with your team to develop steps for future improvement based on specific criteria. Finally, these chapters all include one or more PLC Connection sections we designed to give teams of teachers and administrators practical steps to collaboratively implement standards-based grading.

At the end of the book, you will find two appendixes with a variety of useful resources. Appendix A includes reproducible sets of the standards-based grading continua and action-plan templates. Appendix B has a sample parent-communication letter, sample guidelines other schools have used to establish a common purpose for standards-based grading, and a sample FAQ document schools often use to explain to community stakeholders (such as parents) the benefits of standards-based grading.

A Journey Worth Pursuing

When Matt and I finally finished the phone call that initiated our journey toward standards-based grading at Solon High School, we were committed to creating equitable grading principles for not only the students at the high school but for all students in every school in our district. To achieve this goal, we focused especially on helping our teachers understand these clear standards-based principles for reporting student learning.

In the years that followed our phone conversation, hundreds of teachers have visited Solon High School and other secondary schools in the district to learn about this shift from a classroom perspective. Solon Community School District teachers champion the work of standards-based grading within a PLC. Most important, students no longer come to the principal's office with concerns about grading practices.

The work of developing consistent grading principles has ensured students have a guaranteed and viable instructional experience, which is a major premise of a PLC. In other words, teachers all working together in a common course or grade have common curricular expectations and grading practices for students. We have also seen evidence of more targeted teacher instruction, improved ownership of student learning, and more meaningful communication with parents at home.

Although our secondary students already performed above the state average before this change in grading practices, our achievement continued to improve as we implemented them. When analyzing our student-achievement data, we compared cohorts (grades) of students from the year before implementing standards-based grading to the first year *all* teachers were using standards-based grading. Across the four content areas assessed (reading, mathematics, science, and social studies) in three grade levels, eleven out of twelve cohorts saw improvements in the overall percentage of proficient students that ranged from 0.8–14.8 percent. The average cohort growth was 5.2 percent more student proficiency on statewide assessment than the year prior.

But we didn't simply rely on measures of academic success to measure our improvement. Another measure of success we used was a survey administered throughout the state of Iowa. This survey focused on Safe and Supportive Schools (Hogan, 2011; National Center on Safe Supportive Learning Environments, n.d.). Our data from this survey showed a positive result in the adult-to-student interaction with a measure of 3.45. For context, a score above 3.25 indicates that a school has fostered a healthy climate with optimal conditions for learning in the areas of safety, engagement, and environment.

At the time of our phone call, other schools in our area were not engaged in this work at the secondary level, so we had no one we could turn to. By reading this book, your leadership, teacher, and implementation teams will have a resource to guide them. The tools, steps, and support we provide will help them successfully lay the foundation for implementing standards-based grading and navigate the inevitable challenges along the way. Where many standards-based grading resources offer theory without actionable ideas for teachers and administrators, our book provides those ideas and ultimately leads you toward implementing much-needed grading reform in your secondary schools.

The following chapters will not eliminate all the bumps and bruises of a second-order change such as this (that is, a change that creates a new way of seeing things); however, they will offer practitioner-tested guidance—including quotes and stories from Solon Community School District teachers—as to how secondary educators can make the shift to standards-based grading within a PLC.

CHAPTER 1

Standards-Based Grading in a Professional Learning Community

In *Revisiting Professional Learning Communities at Work*, Richard DuFour, Rebecca DuFour, and Robert Eaker (2008) share the story of Peter Miller, a teacher who started his career teaching secondary social studies. The chapter shows how he transitions from a school where everyone teaches in isolation to one that values collaboration through the PLC process. He is surprised to find out the teachers at his new school are more concerned with ensuring all students learn at a high level than with having their autonomy. As readers, we observe how Peter's increasing collaboration with his coworkers improves his instruction as well as his *assessment literacy*, which the book defines as one's ability to answer the question, "How will we know our students are learning?" (DuFour et al., 2008, p. 215). This is relevant to us in that the grading practices most closely aligned with those of Peter Miller's new school are what many educational writers call *standards-based grading* (O'Connor, 2018; Schimmer, Hillman, & Stalets, 2018; Townsley, 2018).

When the teachers on the district curriculum leadership team at Solon High School read Peter Miller's story for the first time in their collaborative meetings, their immediate reaction was, "How can we implement these ideas here, through our PLC?" Rather than continuing to have content emphasis, assessment, and grading practices that students experienced depend on their teacher—which created an educational lottery for students—our teachers embarked on a multiyear journey toward redefining learning in their schools. This quest to maximize teacher collaboration and understand how to best instruct students on the learning standards they needed to achieve naturally produced changes to grading policies. For example, teachers started to communicate students' current levels of learning in the gradebook based on standards rather than via tests, quizzes, or projects. In addition, teachers continued to report homework completion in the gradebook; however, there was no point value attached to it.

To help your school or district begin or continue this work, in this chapter, we fully introduce the concept and core principles of standards-based grading, their connection to the three big ideas of work within a PLC, and how they align with the four critical questions of a PLC (DuFour et al., 2016).

A Definition of Standards-Based Grading

Although education experts have suggested several nuances in standards-based grading implementation over the years, we find that most agree standards-based grading is a philosophy founded on a consistent set of core principles (Iamarino, 2014; O'Connor, 2018; Schimmer et al., 2018; Townsley, 2018; Vatterott, 2015). The three principles we established in this book's introduction derive from these works.

1. Grades should communicate students' current levels of learning based on standards.

2. Homework should serve as ungraded practice.

3. Students should have multiple opportunities to demonstrate their learning.

These principles guide our exploration of standards-based learning throughout chapters 2–4, but to understand the full scope and impact of this philosophy, we need to dig a little deeper first. In the following sections, we take a thorough look at each of the three principles of standards-based grading.

Standards-Based Grading Principle 1

The information teachers share in a standards-based gradebook or report card looks much different to parents and students than does a points-based system. In a traditional classroom, teachers base grades on a combination of factors, such as student effort, work habits, and academic performance (McMillan, 2001; McMillan, Myran, & Workman, 2002). Teachers often award these points based on sources such as homework completion, quiz scores, drafts of essays, projects, and tests. When parents and students log in to the online gradebook, they frequently read information such as "44 of 50 points reported on a test." As such, those reading the gradebook cannot identify specific areas of proficiency and areas for growth. This is especially troubling if a support staff member or parent desires to help a student improve his or her understanding of the course. Standards-based gradebooks, on the other hand, communicate students' current levels of learning based on clear and understandable standards rather than point accumulation. To communicate learning levels, we suggest that teachers use an agreed-on integer scale (0–4, for example) in association with multiple standards related to the unit or learning goal. We describe this system in more detail in chapter 2 (page 28).

To better understand the value of clear learning standards, consider the following example from a mathematics classroom in which the teacher is explaining the value of standards-based grading to her students. In this example, the mathematics teacher asks students in her class, who are also involved in band, to share the feedback they receive from their band instructor. Rose, the second-chair flute player, tells the teacher that her band instructor, Mr. C., often provides her specific guidance, such as, "Rhythm could be better, but you're exceptional at hitting high notes." With the teacher's guidance, the students then observe how this language emphasizes their learning based on standards, as opposed to point accumulation. In a point-focused system, the student might only hear, "You got a fourteen out of fifteen on your playing test." This comparison leads to a classwide conversation about the similar type of point-focused feedback high school students typically receive on mathematics tests.

Following a weeklong discussion about the merits of having clear standards in grading, the mathematics teacher decides to give her geometry students feedback on each course standard when she hands back the next unit test, rather than merely providing a percentage of points the students earned. For consistency, she also uses student- and parent-friendly language to communicate current levels of learning based on standards in the online gradebook, so these students and their parents can identify ongoing areas of strength and areas where improvement is needed. For example, rather than using the entire state or national standard as written, such as *Given a rectangle, parallelogram, trapezoid, or regular polygon, describe the rotations and reflections that carry it onto itself* (HSG.CO.A.3; National Governors Association Center for Best Practices [NGA] & Council of Chief State School Officers [CCSSO], 2010b), it would be rewritten in parent- and student-friendly language. In the electronic gradebook, parents might instead read, *I understand rotations and reflections of polygons*. These changes helped the students at Solon High School to be more in tune with their learning needs, enabling them to ask questions, such as, "How can I do better on rotations of regular polygons?" instead of, "How do I improve my grade on the unit 3 geometry test?"

Standards-Based Grading Principle 2

Point-focused grading is not just a hindrance to understanding learning goals. A typical practice in secondary schools is requiring students to complete daily home-work assignments. After reviewing their answers in class, the teacher goes through each assignment to make corrections. He or she assigns each assignment a point value and records it in the gradebook. Often, teachers assign this point value based on criteria such as completion, showing work, and following directions, and many secondary teachers regularly punish students for missing homework by deducting them in ways unrelated to students' learning (Vatterott, 2018).

In this scenario, points for homework are based on *doing* rather than *learning*. In some ways, this seems appropriate if the purpose of homework is to allow students to practice and learn from mistakes. Yet, students and parents receive mixed messages in a typical electronic gradebook when they see homework summatively assessed in the same manner as traditional summative assessments, such as tests and projects, which are typically based on the *amount* of content learned. Just as incompatible with positive learning outcomes, when teachers assign points for homework completion or accuracy, students have a natural temptation to chase points, even if it comes at the expense of actually learning the material. Perhaps even more disheartening, students might copy a classmate or have a family member complete practice opportunities assigned for completion outside of class. Rather than assigning a point value to home-work, standards-based grading asks that secondary teachers repurpose homework as ungraded practice and communicate it as such in the electronic gradebook.

A sports analogy illustrates why practice work should not count toward the final grade in a standards-based gradebook. Think of a football coach with an incredible reputation, one who has won the state title four years in a row. This coach has incred-ibly detailed and purposeful plans for each practice session between football games, but it's also common for players to not perform well during practices. Sometimes they excel at executing plays, and sometimes they struggle or even fail outright. Yet, a poor practice does not show up on the scoreboard prior to each game's kickoff. The score for every contest begins 0–0.

In the same manner, teachers should not penalize students in the classroom for practicing their learning poorly. In place of assigning a point value for completed or accurate homework, teachers document completion in the standards-based gradebook with symbols and such notations as *collected, missing, late,* and *absent.* This informa-tion allows parents and students to see what practice work students are completing separately from their assessment grades, which describe students' current level of understanding relative to course standards.

Standards-Based Grading Principle 3

The final principle of standards-based grading requires that students receive multiple opportunities to demonstrate their understanding because students learn at different rates. Consider a traditional class in which student scores entered in the gradebook are permanent. Occasionally, teachers might provide students with opportunities to redo or retake an assessment for partial credit; however, this practice does not support the idea that students' learning takes place at different rates, depending on each student. Instead, teachers should encourage students to continually revise their work to demonstrate increased levels of learning during a reporting period. Through standards-based grading, teacher teams in a PLC work together to meet the needs of each student, ensuring that learning is the constant and time is the variable (DuFour et al., 2016).

Imagine a student named Bobby who struggles to understand stoichiometry (the study of chemical reactions) even after completing a series of assigned worksheets. His frustration grows after a Wednesday quiz in which he successfully answers only half the problems. Meanwhile, his classmate Suzy aces the same worksheets and the quiz.

Following a Thursday after-school tutorial with the chemistry teacher, Bobby has a lightbulb moment in which he fully grasps the concept. Bobby and Suzy both ace the unit test. In this scenario, both students have shown mastery of the learning standards, yet in a classroom with traditional grading, these two students earn different cumulative grades due to the differences in their learning progression. In effect, this punishes students for not knowing or understanding a topic after the first attempt, whether that attempt constituted homework, a quiz, or a test. If the goal is to ensure learning for all students, then grading practices must encourage all students to persist in their knowledge acquisition. A standards-based system prioritizes student learning and allows flexibility for students who learn in different ways and on different days.

Now consider a third student, Jojo, who fails the unit test that Bobby and Suzy ace, but later takes advantage of the same enlightening tutorial session the chemistry teacher offered to Bobby. Standards-based grading permits students like Jojo to work toward mastery by offering them subsequent opportunities to demonstrate understanding beyond the initial all-class assessment. Upon demonstrating a level of mastery similar to Bobby's and Suzy's, Jojo receives a mark in the gradebook for the unit test similar to the other two students', regardless of the time in which each student provided evidence of learning. Again, this is the essence of the PLC process that learning must be the constant and time the variable. When students such as Jojo and Bobby have multiple opportunities to demonstrate their understanding, teachers in a PLC are better able to implement their belief that all students can learn at high levels.

The Three Big Ideas of a PLC

Three big ideas drive all PLCs: (1) all students can learn at high levels, (2) teachers must work together to meet the needs of each student, and (3) schools must demonstrate a results orientation (DuFour et al., 2016). We established this concept in the introduction to this book, but let's more thoroughly examine each of these in relation to the three principles for standards-based grading.

A highly functioning PLC is comprised of collaborative teacher teams who share students and content. The construction of these teams can be highly variable and should be determined based on the school's or district's needs. For example, teams of teachers at Solon High School and Solon Middle School were organized vertically by content area, such as having a high school mathematics team, a middle school science team, and a secondary special education team. Larger schools might organize their collaborative teacher teams by a specific course, such as having a teacher team dedicated to U.S. history instruction. No matter the team construction, to ensure the success of the first big idea, teams of teachers need to focus their work on the four critical questions of a PLC:

1. What knowledge, skills, and dispositions should every student acquire as a result of this unit, this course, or this grade level?
2. How will we know when each student has acquired the essential knowledge and skills?
3. How will we respond when some students do not learn?
4. How will we extend the learning for students who are already proficient? (DuFour et al., 2016, p. 36)

Because secondary collaborative teacher teams believe that all students can learn at high levels (the first big idea), they start by identifying the most important knowledge, skills, and dispositions every student should acquire upon completion of the course (the first critical question). If two biology teachers do not teach the same standards in their courses, it will be challenging to determine if students have learned at high levels. Once teams have determined the most important standards, the next step is to create assessments that help teachers discern which students have acquired these skills so that team members may respond collectively. When assessments are clear and based on the standards, collaborative teacher teams can more effectively work toward ensuring all students will learn at high levels.

The second big idea is that teachers must work together to meet the needs of each student. Teacher teams must have regular time to collaborate, and they must have accountability for work products that indicate they are working toward answering the four critical questions. Providing ninety minutes for teams of teachers to collaborate each week is not enough. Instead, collaborative teams must prioritize their standards within a given timeframe. Likewise, teacher teams need to create and administer common formative assessments each quarter to illustrate their commitment to meeting the needs of each student. Through this loose–tight leadership style (DuFour, 2007), teacher teams are held accountable while receiving the flexibility they need to work toward the four critical questions throughout the school year.

The third big idea involves having a results orientation to determine if the school is meeting the needs of all students. Think of this as establishing a system for collecting evidence of learning. For example, teams of teachers in a PLC often demonstrate a results orientation by establishing SMART goals (strategic and specific, measurable, attainable, results oriented, and time bound; Conzemius & O'Neill, 2014) and evaluating every new school program's documented impact on student learning. For example, a science team might set a goal of increasing test scores on the state exam by 10 percent at the end of the school year. In working toward this goal, the team creates common formative assessments aligned with the standards assessed on the state exam. Using the information collected from this formative assessment data, teachers have evidence of their effectiveness and specific areas for instructional change during the school year to maximize the potential of meeting their team's end-of-year SMART goal.

When these teacher teams begin to work together using a results orientation, it draws attention toward students' current levels of learning related to standards, which may bring up questions about grading. These questions might sound something like, "If we are more interested in *all* students' learning at high levels, why should we continue to deduct points for late work?" and "Because we want to identify quickly the students who have learned, why would we continue reporting points, percentages, and test scores when we could instead report on the standards themselves?" This book will help teachers answer these questions by offering a framework for how to implement it and establishing how the principles of standards-based grading align with the four critical questions of a PLC.

Standards-Based Grading Principles and the Four Critical Questions of a PLC

Collaborative teacher teams in the midst of determining the knowledge, skills, and dispositions students should know in their course or grade level may discuss why these same standards are not being communicated in the electronic gradebook in place of points and percentages. Similarly, teachers implementing standards-based grading will find it necessary to prioritize standards and develop assessments collaboratively with their teams rather than in isolation. In both cases, standards-based grading and PLCs work hand in hand. Table 1.1 illustrates how the three principles of standards-based grading and the four critical questions of PLCs align.

In reflecting on the alignment between PLC critical questions and standards-based grading principles, consider how a typical secondary school may often spend time assisting students who are currently on a list of students earning Ds and Fs in one or more of their courses. Although these students have poor grades in common, the reasons for those poor outcomes are sure to be plentiful. One student may be putting forth a tremendous amount of effort, yet still has not yet demonstrated understanding on a civics test, which results in a failing grade. Another student may not be motivated to turn in any assignments at all, which also results in a failing grade. Secondary schools should respond to the needs of these two students who have not yet learned in different ways. When a secondary PLC is working toward standards-based grading, grappling with scenarios like this one, it inherently mandates that collaborative teams are also answering the four critical questions. We describe this important work in the following sections.

PLC Critical Questions 1 and 2

When a team of teachers begins to answer PLC critical question 1 (What knowledge must students acquire?) and PLC critical question 2 (How will we know when they have acquired it?), a natural next step is to begin implementing the first standards-based grading principle (Grades should communicate students' current levels of learning based on standards). In other words, once a teacher team determines what students should be learning and agrees on how the teachers will know if each student has learned it, the team takes the step of communicating students' current levels of learning in the gradebook.

Typically, teams of teachers in a PLC meet regularly to determine the essential standards or targets students must learn. In addition, these teams of educators create

Table 1.1: Connections Between the Four PLC Critical Questions and Standards-Based Grading Principles

Critical Questions of a PLC	Standards-Based Grading Principles		
	1. Grades should communicate students' current levels of learning based on standards.	2. Homework should serve as ungraded practice.	3. Students should have multiple opportunities to demonstrate their learning.
1. What knowledge, skills, and dispositions should every student acquire as a result of this unit, this course, or this grade level?	✓	✓	
2. How will we know when each student has acquired the essential knowledge and skills?	✓	✓	
3. How will we respond when some students do not learn?	✓	✓	✓
4. How will we extend the learning for students who are already proficient?	✓		

Source: DuFour et al., 2016.

and administer assessments they feel will enable them to know if each student has learned these essential standards. At the culmination of a unit of study, teachers who follow traditional grading practices often enter the results of a test, project, or essay as a single point-based score in the gradebook. Rather than communicating learning to parents and students through a single point-based score, teachers in a standards-based grading classroom communicate learning using an agreed-on integer scale. This scale represents the student's current level of learning relative to the standard the team determined in answering PLC critical question 1. You will learn more about this in chapter 2 (page 21).

Homework also plays an important role in giving students feedback on the agreed-on standards; however, its purpose is practice, not an expectation of mastery. Therefore, teachers should record in the gradebook whether students completed homework, but they should not assign grades or otherwise use homework for grading purposes. When teachers do need to record homework scores, they should base these numbers on whether students completed the assignments in question. Chapter 3 (page 47) explains this dynamic in greater detail.

PLC Critical Questions 3 and 4

After teacher teams have determined what they want students to learn and how they will know each student has learned it (PLC critical questions 1 and 2), they next need to address PLC critical questions 3 and 4. These questions require that teams determine how to collectively respond when students have not yet learned curricula content and how to extend and enrich the learning for those students who have demonstrated proficiency.

Through standards-based grading principle 1, communicating students' current levels of learning based on standards, teachers can explicitly identify the areas where students have not yet learned as well as the areas where they have already demonstrated proficiency. Thus, the gradebook serves as a scoreboard of sorts, not for points, but for collaborative teams to identify, standard by standard, those areas where students demonstrate excellence or a need for growth (Buffum, Mattos, & Weber, 2012).

At the end of a unit of study, when a teacher team determines which students have not yet demonstrated proficiency, as measured by a summative assessment that it documents in a standards-based gradebook, the team faces an interesting dilemma. Students have had ample time to practice, and the test deadline has come and gone, yet not all students have demonstrated understanding, so the team's desire to meet all students' needs while ensuring they all learn at high levels remains unfulfilled.

These students need additional time and support within the reporting period. As such, the third standards-based grading principle—providing students with multiple opportunities to demonstrate understanding—helps teachers walk the talk of ensuring learning as the constant and time as the variable. See chapter 4 (page 71) for more on implementing this principle.

Before implementing standards-based grading, teachers can find it difficult to identify students who have already demonstrated proficiency (PLC critical question 4) before a unit of study ends. When teachers see a *100 percent* in the gradebook, it does not tell them the specific standards the student has mastered, whereas teachers can easily identify which students have demonstrated proficiency when the gradebook documents students' current levels of understanding based on specific standards. Being able to quickly and easily identify those students enables teachers to plan ways they can use ungraded homework (standards-based grading principle 2) to enrich and extend the students' learning. For example, in a mathematics class at Solon High School, a small group of students often completed all assigned homework problems with ease and wanted a greater challenge. They had shared their concern with the teacher as they were approaching the ACT test date. The teacher encouraged the students to extend their learning by developing practice ACT test questions that aligned with the mathematics content in the course. The students then worked to create video examples of these problems and shared these with classmates for each other to review.

Assessment Tools for Your Journey

This chapter started with introducing the concept and core principles of standards-based grading and the three big ideas of work within a PLC. Toward the end of the chapter, we illustrated and explained the inherent connections between the three standards-based grading principles and the four critical questions of a PLC. Prior to considering standards-based grading, a PLC will benefit from knowing how its previous work implementing the three big ideas and four critical questions is a natural progression, rather than a step in a new direction. Figure 1.1 (page 18) offers teams an organizer to visualize their answers to the four critical questions and connect those answers to the standards-based grading principles. Departments, leadership teams, and entire schools may use the self-reported answers to plan their next implementation supports.

Now that you know about standards-based grading and how the PLC process provides the perfect foundation for implementation, the next three chapters will each

Directions: As a team, respond to each of the four critical questions of a PLC and provide evidence supporting your response. Next, suggest how the current critical question responses may be connected to one or more standards-based grading principles.

Critical Questions of a PLC	How does our team currently respond to this question?	What connections can our team make to one or more of the standards-based grading principles?
1. What knowledge, skills, and dispositions should every student acquire as a result of this unit, this course, or this grade level?		"Grades should communicate students' current levels of learning based on standards." Our possible team connection is . . . "Homework should serve as ungraded practice." Our possible team connection is . . .
2. How will we know when each student has acquired the essential knowledge and skills?		"Grades should communicate students' current levels of learning based on standards." Our possible team connection is . . . "Homework should serve as ungraded practice." Our possible team connection is . . .

3. How will we respond when some students do not learn?	"Grades should communicate students' current levels of learning based on standards." Our possible team connection is . . . "Homework should serve as ungraded practice." Our possible team connection is . . . "Students should have multiple opportunities to demonstrate their learning." Our possible connection is . . .
4. How will we extend the learning for students who are already proficient?	"Grades should communicate students' current levels of learning based on standards." Our possible team connection is . . .

Source: DuFour et al., 2016.

Figure 1.1: Organizer to align the four critical questions of a PLC with standards-based grading principles.

Visit go.SolutionTree.com/PLCbooks for a free reproducible version of this figure.

focus on implementing one of the three core grading principles. We describe each standards-based grading principle in detail, explain how to implement it individually as well as within a PLC, and offer common hurdles to avoid. Each subsequent chapter's closing Assessment Tools for Your Journey section also introduces specific standards-based grading continua to assist individual teachers and teams of teachers in implementing that principle. These continua will help you and your team take your next steps on the road toward standards-based grading.

CHAPTER 2

How Grades Communicate Current Levels of Learning

Gradebooks usually include summative measures of learning (tests, projects, and essays); however, the resulting points and percentage scores do not always communicate students' strengths and weaknesses relative to academic content taught in the course (Guskey, 2013). Because teachers in a PLC strive to ensure all students learn at a high level, it is important that the data in their gradebooks explicitly communicate students' mastery of learning standards, rather than points or percentages. An 85 percent test score does not describe to a parent or student the explicit areas in which the learner has mastered standards or needs to improve. Furthermore, when a student's final course grade includes points from nonacademic factors (such as class participation and work habits) and formative assessments (such as homework, quizzes, and exit slips), the grade becomes foggy and may not accurately communicate a student's *current* level of understanding. In his article "Grading to Communicate," Tony Winger (2005) tells educators, "When grades are not deliberately connected to learning, they provide little valuable feedback regarding students' academic strengths and weaknesses, and can even be counterproductive" (p. 62).

Ask educators to identify which scenario might describe a student who currently has an 85 percent (B) in their classroom, and they could have a variety of responses.

- "The student understands 85 percent of the course's main ideas."

- "The student understands 100 percent of the course's main ideas but didn't turn in 15 percent of the assignments."

- "The student understands 90 percent of the course's main ideas but turned in one or more assignments late."

- "The student understands 75 percent of the course's main ideas but turned in a few extra-credit assignments, raising his or her grade to 85 percent."

More than likely, educators will identify with more than one of these scenarios. When teachers describe what makes the difference between earning a B and earning a C in their class, possible responses often remain highly variable.

- "That's easy—about 10 percent of the points."

- "A B student has earned more points on assignments than a C student."

- "A student in my class who earns a B has completed more work on time than the C student. On tests and homework, the B student demonstrated a higher understanding of concepts and skills learned in class than the C student."

- "A B student does what I ask and scores at the average on tests. A C student doesn't always do what I ask as a teacher and scores at the average on my tests."

These two discussion starters and sets of common responses vividly suggest that the factors influencing student grades vary widely from classroom to classroom. In one survey of California teachers, 93 percent of respondents included homework submission, not accuracy, in determining the final course grade (Campbell, 2012). In this same survey, nearly 30 percent of teachers included a student's behavior, attendance, or their perception of the student when calculating the final course grade. None of these factors are directly related to how much learning students have demonstrated, which is a problem if parents, colleges and universities, and future employers are assuming letter grades communicate academic mastery. In addition, students benefit from seeing their assessments disaggregated. Rather than a score of 70 out of 100, reporting out on the topic or standard allows students to understand their specific strengths and areas for improvement (Marzano & Heflebower, 2011).

What, then, is the alternative to traditional practices that often yield such inconsistent communication? In *A Repair Kit for Grading*, Ken O'Connor (2007) suggests the following:

> Teachers should use learning goals as the basis for determining grades. . . . They provide a profile of a student's knowledge and direct evidence of his or her strengths and weaknesses. This type of assessment allows teachers to appropriately plan instruction and allows students to focus their learning. (p. 231)

As you may have intuited already, this statement lies at the heart of the first standards-based grading principle—grades should communicate current levels of learning based on standards. In this chapter, we explore four criteria for successfully implementing this principle in your school or district. In addition, this chapter explains how to connect this principle to your work within a PLC, describes common pitfalls to avoid, and provides a standards-based grading continuum and an action-plan template to help you assess your journey and determine next steps in implementing this grading principle.

Four Criteria for Communicating Students' Current Learning

When a team of teachers starts answering the first and second critical questions of a PLC, the team's natural next step is to implement standards-based grading principle 1. In other words, once teams working in a PLC decide what students should learn and how they will know if each student has learned it (DuFour et al., 2016), teams should clearly communicate students' current levels of learning in the gradebook. This next step makes sense; however, communicating students' levels of learning based on standards is not always an easy task. Let's further describe this challenge and how leadership teams and administrators can support teachers in this mindset change.

Moving from a gradebook or report card that tracks a combination of student behaviors, participation, attendance, homework completion, and test scores to one primarily focused on standards is a paradigm shift that assumes all stakeholders have a common understanding of the purpose of grades. But teachers should not make this assumption. Instead, before transitioning to standards-based grading, collaborative teams should foster a common understanding of the purpose of grading and standards-based grading reform. Educational consultant and author Susan M. Brookhart (2011) suggests initially engaging stakeholders in various belief statements about grading.

Belief statements help identify a school staff's convictions about grading. Facilitating discussion to identify beliefs can also help a school leader or leadership team identify potential obstacles for staff members that may lead to future roadblocks. For example, let's say staff have a collective belief that grades should differentiate students and schools should sort students based on who is succeeding in their learning and who is not. This stated belief will help the leader or leadership team inform, educate, and mitigate future barriers that may arise due to the sorting of students. It creates a question to address before moving forward with a full standards-based grading implementation.

As teams review questions arising from belief statements, school leaders may find Thomas R. Guskey's (2011) five obstacles to grading reform helpful as they work with various groups during this transition phase. These obstacles represent baked-in preconceptions we often see in teachers new to the concept of standards-based grading. For educators leading a shift toward standards-based grading, knowing how to recognize these obstacles enables those leaders to mitigate them. The first three obstacles Guskey (2011) notes are the beliefs that (1) grades should serve as a means to differentiate students, (2) grades should resemble a bell-shaped curve, and (3) grades should be based on students' standing relative to their peers. Guskey (2015a) suggests that overcoming these obstacles requires educators to ask, "What is the purpose of school? Is it to develop talent or select talent?"

Educators who seek to develop talent, and in turn foster a growth mindset (Dweck, 2006), believe all students have the potential to learn at a high level and earn high marks. This belief contrasts with educators who are more comfortable sorting talent based on summative assessments and moving on to the next unit or topic even though many students may not have demonstrated understanding of the course standards (yet). Helping educators see the purpose of school as developing talent is a necessary step in identifying the purpose of grades and overcoming these three obstacles. It is also one of the three big ideas of a PLC—ensuring all students learn at high levels (DuFour et al., 2016).

The fourth obstacle Guskey (2011) notes is the myth that poor grades prompt students to try harder. Although no research supports this myth, an observation of high school gradebooks quickly validates that teachers maintain this misconception. Ask a veteran seventh-grade teacher to identify a dozen current seniors he or she assigned low grades during their seventh-grade year. Now, ask a current high school teacher who teaches those same students as twelfth graders to identify a dozen students with low grades. Chances are, the students who received low grades for the sake of motivation in middle school are the same ones not feeling motivated to improve as seniors (and that's if they haven't dropped out already).

If poor grades prompted students to try harder, poor grades would occur at a minimum frequency among students who have been in the system the longest because they would have learned a lesson and improved going forward. When educators understand the purpose of grades is to develop talent and report students' current strengths and weaknesses through the gradebook, our experience suggests they are more likely to seek out motivational methods beyond extra credit and point accumulation.

The final obstacle Guskey (2011) notes is the idea many educators have that students should receive one grade for each subject or course. Traditional grading conversations between parents and teachers focus on deciphering the underlying reason for the grade. Did Johnny earn a C because he is not putting forth effort in class, because he doesn't understand the material, or because he has turned in several assignments late? At the heart of standards-based grading is communicating students' current levels of learning and repurposing homework as ungraded practice (the topic of chapter 3, page 47). When teachers report current levels of learning separately from ungraded practice, they can quickly identify students who have not yet learned as well as those who need enrichment or extension, which aligns with the third and fourth critical questions of a PLC (DuFour et al., 2016). Similarly, communicating dynamic indicators of a student's current level of understanding separate from ungraded practice makes the purpose of grades clearer to all.

Overcoming these obstacles is a challenge. As educational leadership experts Randal Peters and Tom Buckmiller (2014) suggest, "The adoption and implementation of standards-based grading is a difficult endeavor, even under optimal conditions." Following adequate discussion on the purpose of grades, educators and parents need to agree that grades should primarily reflect students' learning and that standards are the most appropriate way to reflect their learning in the gradebook or report card.

The following sections thoroughly describe the four criteria needed to ensure that grades communicate students' current levels of learning based on standards.

1. Numbers in the gradebook should reflect understanding of standards rather than assessment task grades.

2. All standards should derive from state, provincial, or national standards.

3. The number of standards in the gradebook should be manageable for teachers.

4. Teachers should rewrite standards so parents and students can understand them.

Numbers in the Gradebook Should Reflect Understanding of Standards Rather Than Assessment Task Grades

Before we look at standards-based gradebooks, it is important to understand the challenges of traditional (points-based) gradebooks, which most teachers use. The traditional gradebook in a classroom without standards-based grading, as figure 2.1 (page 26) illustrates, communicates how many points a student earned on assessment tasks, such as homework assignments, quizzes, projects, and tests for each unit of study. In an era of instant internet updates, parents often have access to teachers' electronic gradebooks online and in real time.

English Language Arts		
Date	**Assignment or Task**	**Score**
9/15	Test 1	20/20
9/20	Worksheet 1	5/5
9/25	Rough draft of essay	10/10
10/15	Second draft of essay	17/20
10/20	Worksheet 2	5/5
10/30	Final draft of essay	12/20

Figure 2.1: Assessment task–based gradebook.

For as long as online access to student information has existed, school leaders have trained parents to play an active role in their child's learning by logging in to check grades. Some student information systems automatically email daily and weekly reports to parents that the online gradebook generates. Students are also able to access their assignment and assessment scores in real time. One sixth-grade student describes his experience with the PowerSchool student information system:

> At first, I found myself logging on to the system every other day to check my most recent test scores. But as the school year went on, I found myself logging on every night to check my grades and to make sure I hadn't missed any homework assignments for that night. The system certainly helped keep me current on my assignments and grades. (Bazemore, 2006)

We can best describe the traditional online gradebook as a timeline of tasks written in ink. That is, scores entered are static. Teachers may award points for following their directions on tasks, such as merely completing a homework assignment and turning it in by the deadline, regardless of the accuracy or depth of knowledge the student's work demonstrates. Such completion grades provide parents a reason to ask questions such as, "Why didn't you turn in that worksheet?" and "How long have you known about the chapter 7 review questions?"

Guskey (2002) reminds educators why the simplistic record-keeping in traditional online gradebooks is a problem:

> Computerized grading programs and electronic gradebooks greatly simplify the record-keeping tasks teachers face. They allow teachers to collect and efficiently summarize large amounts

of data on student learning. But the efficiency and mathematical precision of these programs does not make the grades they generate more accurate, honest, fair, or objective. (p. 780)

To reiterate a passage from the start of this section, teacher teams in a PLC must understand the strengths and limitations of electronic gradebooks and how they communicate data about students' learning. For example, the points and percentages these electronic gradebooks typically display do not transparently communicate a student's strengths and areas of improvement relative to standards. When transitioning to standards-based grading, teacher teams should be able to look at the gradebook and answer the critical question, How will we know when each student has learned it? Through the gradebook, they should be able to identify, by student and by standard, who learned what. For students who didn't learn, the next question is, Why?

As teachers begin to analyze their students' progress in regard to standards, it will be important to separate students with *skill* gaps from students with *will* gaps. Buffum et al. (2012) refer to this as identifying academic misbehaviors as separate from social misbehaviors. Skill gaps often show up when students are completing the homework and classroom assignments but, when assessed on the standard, they fail to reach proficiency. Will gaps are often present in students that simply refuse or are unmotivated to do the work. Causes of this behavior can take many forms. Ultimately, teachers need to recognize these differences as the intervention methods for addressing skill and will gaps should be different.

Note that the example standards-based gradebook in figure 2.2 (page 28) includes standards and corresponding indicators for the student. Practice assignments are also documented; however, unique marks separate them from standards that count toward the final grade. (We detail the purpose for this in chapter 3, page 47.) This permits teachers to note students who have not yet demonstrated understanding but who are completing homework and practice assignments as those with a skill gap to fill. Similarly, teachers can assist students who have not yet demonstrated an understanding of one or more course standards and have not turned in many homework and practice assignments with their will gap. The student represented in figure 2.2 has not yet turned in the reading response practice (worksheet 4), which may suggest why he or she has not successfully completed tasks related to analyzing an author's claims and determining an author's point of view. (Note that the standards listed in this example, and others throughout the book, are generic and not derived from a specific source.)

English Language Arts		
Date	**Practice or Standard**	**Score**
9/8	Practice: Worksheet 1	✓
9/15	Standard: Identify the theme or central idea of a text.	4
9/22	Practice: Worksheet 2	L
10/1	Standard: Cite evidence to support analysis.	3
10/8	Practice: Worksheet 3	✓
10/14	Standard: Write arguments to support analysis.	4
10/21	Practice: Worksheet 4	X
10/30	Standard: Analyze the author's claims.	2
10/30	Standard: Determine the author's point of view.	1
Homework and practice key: ✓ = Collected X = Missing L = Late Ab = Absent	**Assessment key:** 0 = No evidence of learning 1 = Minimal understanding 2 = Partial understanding 3 = Proficiency with standards 4 = Mastery of standards	

Figure 2.2: Standards-based gradebook.

As figure 2.2 shows, rather than using abstract collections of points, teachers in a standards-based classroom communicate current levels of learning using a key-based integer scale. While teachers may use any number of levels on a scale, those levels should clearly describe the differences in student learning. Figure 2.2 lists a five-level scale (0–4) with each level clearly defined. Some secondary teachers may be hesitant to use zeros in the gradebook based on the advice of other grading experts who suggest eliminating its use on a one hundred–point scale. We concur with Douglas Reeves (2004) in that we believe using a zero *on a four- or five-level scale* can be appropriate to report no evidence of learning following multiple attempts to assist the student in completing his or her culminating assessment.

This type of scoring also matches that of a *holistic rubric*—a rubric designed with three to five levels of performance along with a broad description that defines each level (Balch, Blanck, & Balch, 2016). Holistic scoring allows parents and students to recognize how close the students are to understanding the standard. In addition, by analyzing the list of standards in the gradebook as well as students' levels of proficiency with the standards, teachers can use this information to answer the first and second critical questions of a PLC.

In an ideal world, teachers would transfer the numbers communicating students' current levels of learning on the standards directly from the gradebook to the report card, regardless of the grade level. (In other words, there would be no need to assign a traditional letter grade.) Some middle schools do choose to report the standards directly on report cards, rather than determining a letter grade for each course. However, admissions processes at institutions of higher learning often require high school transcripts to include letter grades and grade point averages. As such, at the end of each grading period, high school teachers using standards-based grading determine letter grades, which they base on the integers that communicate students' current levels of learning for each standard in the gradebook. Chapter 5 (page 103) offers an example of this process.

We can best describe a standards-based gradebook as a thermometer that dynamically communicates students' current levels of learning in relation to the course or grade-level standards. Most important, these levels of learning based on standards are written in pencil. In chapter 4 (page 71), we cover more about the importance of providing students with multiple opportunities to demonstrate their learning and replacing old evidence of learning with new evidence of learning in the gradebook.

All Standards Should Derive From State, Provincial, or National Standards

Once a team of teachers determines what students should be learning and agrees on how it will know if each student has learned it (PLC critical questions 1 and 2), the next step is to decide how to determine the standards that go into the gradebook. When teachers find out they should use standards rather than assessment tasks to calculate grades, a natural question for them to ask is, "What standards should we use?" Whether the standards required in a school are state, provincial, or national, all gradebook entries counted toward the final grade or communicated on the report card must connect to these standards.

Some districts may choose to prioritize the standards and rewrite them into parent- and student-friendly language in the gradebook, while others may choose to rewrite the standards into a series of learning targets or another condensed form. In contrast to merely copying and pasting textbook objectives without first conducting a correlative mapping process, utilizing state, provincial, or national standards as the foundation for developing the standards that appear in gradebooks ensures teachers do not compromise the standards' intent. Note that teachers will often find the language in state, provincial, or national standards to be *eduspeak*, meaning that it is difficult for students and parents to understand. The correlative mapping process allows collaborative teams to discuss the complex language of the standards and identify wording to be entered in the gradebook that students and parents will find more accessible.

For example, an algebra 2 textbook objective might read, *Solve real-world systems involving three variables.* A mathematics teacher team in a PLC would need to determine how well this objective aligns with a state, provincial, or national standard, such as, "Prove that, given a system of two equations in two variables, replacing one equation by the sum of that equation and a multiple of the other produces a system with the same solutions" (HSA-REI.C.5; NGA & CCSSO, 2010b). A more student- and parent-friendly version of this standard might read as *Equivalent systems of equations* in the gradebook. Another example standard might be, "Solve systems of linear equations exactly and approximately (e.g., with graphs), focusing on pairs of linear equations in two variables" (HSA-REI.C.6; NGA & CCSSO, 2010b). When mapping this standard to the gradebook, a mathematics team might write it as *Students can solve systems of equations with graphs.* You will learn more about rewriting standards in Teachers Should Rewrite Standards So Parents and Students Can Understand Them (page 32).

At times, teachers may not have enough instructional hours to teach, assess, and reassess *all* the required standards as they appear in the gradebook. In addition, entering assessment results for the standards may take secondary teachers more time than their previous practice of entering a single number for each assessment in the gradebook. The next section emphasizes the importance of making the number of standards in the gradebook manageable.

The Number of Standards in the Gradebook Should Be Manageable for Teachers

Teachers need to find balance in teaching and assessing students based on a manageable number of essential standards and in efficiently communicating their standards-based learning in the gradebook. Entering one score for an end-of-unit test logically takes less time than entering an integer for each standard assessed on the test. Experienced standards-based grading teachers suggest the time they gain from no longer scoring formative assessments, such as homework (more about this in chapter 3, page 47), is quickly filled with additional integer data entry at the end of the unit of study. Jim Erickson, Solon High School English language arts teacher, comments, "At first, I felt like a new teacher all over again. Now, I spend less time tracking down students for their missing grammar worksheets and more effort providing students with standards-specific feedback on their draft essays" (personal communication, September 9, 2013).

While there is no magic number of standards, teacher teams can determine the number of standards they can realistically cover and report in the gradebook. In an interview in *Educational Leadership*, Robert J. Marzano gives educators a powerful reality check: to cover all content in a typical standards document, they would have to add ten years to public education (as cited in Scherer, 2001). We need a more realistic approach. For example, in a 180-day school year, a class may have 155 full days of instruction, after factoring in state assessments, assemblies, pep rallies, and other events. If a class or content area completes twelve units of study with six standards each, teachers must report seventy-two standards in the gradebook. Devoting one and a half days per standard yields 108 days of allotted instructional time. This leaves forty-seven days to more formally assess students and provide them with meaningful feedback opportunities. With less than one day to provide meaningful feedback for each standard, educators find themselves in a precarious position of prioritizing content coverage over ensuring students have actually learned the standards. As such, teams of teachers must determine a manageable number of standards to teach, assess, and reassess during a given reporting period.

To determine this number, teacher teams should consider how many instructional days they will need per standard and add several days per unit so they can check for understanding and assess students' learning. For example, a ninth-grade English teacher, with state standards to meet in reading literature, reading informational text, writing, language, and speaking and listening, may have over sixty standards to cover in a school year. With 180 school days, this is one standard for every three days, which is far too many for the typical teacher to teach well, check for under-standing, and assess with fidelity, let alone engage in intervention or enrichment. As such, PLCs should require a collaborative team of English teachers to prioritize those standards into a condensed and more meaningful list of twenty to thirty standards. This prioritized list would allow the team to identify four to five standards for each five-to-six-week unit of study. The PLC Connection section for this chapter (page 33) provides teacher teams with a process for prioritizing standards in this way.

Note that we share this example to begin a conversation rather than provide a prescription. Teams working in a PLC must consider factors and variables unique to their school or district when determining an ideal set of learning standards. For example, if a high school strongly encourages its students to enroll in advanced-placement courses, the prioritized standards may be vertically aligned, thus building up to these important courses. Similarly, a school with many of its students matriculating to trade programs or community colleges may choose to emphasize standards more in line with their admissions requirements.

Teachers Should Rewrite Standards So Parents and Students Can Understand Them

It is not uncommon for skilled and experienced classroom teachers to feel challenged when reviewing state, provincial, or national learning standards. Consider the following grades 9–10 standard for reading:

> Determine the meaning of words and phrases as they are used in the text, including figurative and connotative meanings; analyze the cumulative impact of specific word choices on meaning and tone (e.g., how the language evokes a sense of time and place; how it sets a formal or informal tone). (RL.9–10.4; NGA & CCSSO, 2010a)

Think about this standard in the context of this chapter's standards-based grading principle—grades should communicate students' current levels of learning based on standards. To accomplish this, teachers and school leaders need time to rewrite standards in a way noneducators can begin to understand. They can do this by answering the following three questions from students' perspective:

1. What will I be able to do when I've finished this lesson?
2. What idea, topic, or subject is important for me to learn and understand so that I can do this?
3. How will I show that I can do this, and how well will I have to do it? (Moss, Brookhart, & Long, 2011, p. 67)

I can statements are an effective way to answer these questions, and they become even more powerful as students begin to more clearly connect their learning with phrases and skills found in the gradebook. For example, consider a state middle school science standard that reads, "Construct a scientific explanation based on evidence for how environmental and genetic factors influence the growth of organisms" (MS-LS1-5; NGSS Lead States, 2013). In the gradebook, the teacher may rewrite it for parents and students as *I can explain environmental and genetic factors using evidence through a classroom presentation.*

Note how all three components suggested in Moss et al., (2011) are evident in this *I can* statement. First, the student is being asked to explain using evidence after they've finished the lesson. This can be met through a variety of assessment practices, such as a skit or a more formal oral presentation. Secondly, the idea or topic the student is focused on is environmental and genetic factors. Finally, the collaborative teacher team will have created performance-level indicators for the student so that he or she is aware of the requirements of the classroom presentation when demonstrating understanding of the *I can* statement.

Converting standards to *I can* statements is also beneficial for teacher teams in a PLC because doing so further clarifies what they want students to learn (the first critical question). Through condensing each standard into one or more *I can* statements, teachers must think deeply about the standard's intent, what the standard means, and what it does not mean.

PLC Connection

Although individual teachers can accomplish a number of the criteria necessary to implement the first standards-based grading principle, teams of teachers working collaboratively within a PLC are best equipped to prioritize which standards will be communicated in the gradebook or report card. Here's why: in a traditional school structure, teachers make important instructional decisions in isolation (DuFour & Marzano, 2011). As the end of each school year approaches, teachers begin to look ahead in their lesson-planning books and decide which content or units they still need to teach and which they will omit. Individual teachers make these prioritization decisions with the best intentions but, in a PLC, these individual decisions do not suffice. A team working within a broader organization (like a PLC), is in a better position to make these decisions. Using a formal process to prioritize standards, a team can ensure that all students receive an equitable learning environment regardless of their instructor. The purpose of this section is to provide teacher teams with practical steps for prioritizing standards as well as suggest a realistic timeline for accomplishing this important work.

When a team meets to consider the first critical question of a PLC—What is it we want our students to learn?—team discussions often turn to identifying the most important standards within state, provincial, or national documents. This process of identifying *priority standards* (also called *power standards*) requires teacher teams to agree on the most important standards for each course or content area (Ainsworth & Viegut, 2006; Crawford, 2011; Reeves, 2000).

Teams can use a three-step process to accomplish this work of determining priority standards.

1. Individual teachers complete the template in figure 2.3 for each standard in their courses that aligns with state, provincial, or national standards documents.

2. Teachers who teach the same grade level, courses, or content area work to reach consensus on the answers to each yes–no question in figure 2.3. During team collaboration time, individual teachers should feel encouraged to share their reasoning for each *yes* or *no*. Because teachers all have their own experiences and perspectives, we advise teams to establish or revisit their team norms before entering into these discussions. There will always be differences of opinion among teachers, but these should not prevent the team from completing the activity. Revisiting norms can help remind collaborative team members what to do when differences of opinion arise during a meeting and how to keep their conversation focused on the agreed-on agenda items.

3. The team uses the consensus yeses and nos for each standard to determine whether it should be a priority standard. Figure 2.4 (page 36) offers a template that teams can use to build a consensus on priority standards.

When reviewing how members answered the yes–no questions, a team should consider the following criteria as a starting point in its conversations for building team consensus.

- If the team answered *yes* in four to five columns, the team should strongly consider the standard as a priority standard.

- If the team answered *yes* in three columns, the team should consider the standard as a priority standard, depending on the number of priority standards it identified. Ideally, we suggest using it as a priority standard on a trial basis in the first year of implementation and then revisiting it for the next school year.

- If the team answered *yes* in fewer than three columns, the team should not consider the standard as a priority standard.

Directions: Select a standard, and use each column to assess whether the standard meets or does not meet the priority-standard criteria found in the column heading. A *yes* in more than three columns indicates this is a priority standard. If there is a *no* in three or more columns, it is likely not a priority standard. Results in between indicate a need to further review and assess the standard's importance.

Standard:							
Teacher Input: Is this standard important to know? Can a student learn the content—the big concept—without having this information? (Circle *yes* or *no*.)		**Endurance:** Do we really expect our students to retain the knowledge and skills over time, as opposed to merely learning them for a test? (Circle *yes* or *no*.)		**Readiness:** Is the standard essential for success in the next unit, course, or grade level? (Circle *yes* or *no*.)		**Leverage:** Will proficiency in this standard help our students in other areas of the curriculum and in other academic disciplines? (Circle *yes* or *no*.)		**State or Provincial and National Testing:** Is the standard tested? (Circle *yes* or *no*.)
Yes	No	Yes	No	Yes	No	Yes	No	Yes	No
My reasoning:		**My reasoning:**		**My reasoning:**		**My reasoning:**		**Number of related questions on the test:**

Source: Adapted from Ainsworth, 2013; Reeves, 2002.

Figure 2.3: Template for identifying priority standards.

*Visit **go.SolutionTree.com/PLCbooks** for a free reproducible version of this figure.*

Standard:										
Teacher Name	**Teacher Input** (Circle *yes* or *no*.)		**Endurance** (Circle *yes* or *no*.)		**Readiness** (Circle *yes* or *no*.)		**Leverage** (Circle *yes* or *no*.)		**State or Provincial and National Testing** (Circle *yes* or *no*.)	
	Yes	No	Yes	No	Yes	No	Yes	No	Yes	No
	Yes	No	Yes	No	Yes	No	Yes	No	Yes	No
	Yes	No	Yes	No	Yes	No	Yes	No	Yes	No
	Yes	No	Yes	No	Yes	No	Yes	No	Yes	No
Consensus	Yes	No	Yes	No	Yes	No	Yes	No	Yes	No
Is this a priority standard? (Circle yes or no.)									Yes	No

Figure 2.4: Template for building team consensus on priority standards.

*Visit **go.SolutionTree.com/PLCbooks** for a free reproducible version of this figure.*

- At the conclusion of this activity, if the team finds too many or too few standards, it should replicate the process with the prioritized list of standards (if too many) or the deprioritized list of standards (if too few). The goal of the team should be to more critically evaluate the list and reduce it to a manageable number or increase it to a suitable number.

One litmus test for discerning if the list of prioritized standards represents a manageable number is to try it out for a school year. If teachers in the collaborative team can adequately teach all of the prioritized standards, check students for understanding, and assess the standards—all while leaving time to reteach or enrich instruction as appropriate—the list is, in practice, manageable.

Completing these steps to identify priority standards puts teams in a much stronger position to address the third criterion of this standards-based grading principle—choosing a number of standards for the gradebook or report card that teachers find manageable. However, teacher teams should also reconsider the final criterion of this grading principle, which requires that they write standards in a way parents and students can understand. Merely copying the priority standards and pasting them into the gradebook or onto the report card does not ensure parents or students will understand them. Teams should pay careful attention to rewording the priority standards, so parents and students easily understand them.

Even in the most experienced teams, it may take considerable time to prioritize the standards for each course or content area. We suggest leadership teams in a PLC establish a reasonable timeline for this important work. For example, some leadership teams may require teachers in the same grade or content area to spend an entire year collaboratively prioritizing the standards. In year 2, teacher teams might go through a process of vertical articulation, after teachers have taught the priority standards to students. Although, after a few years of trial and error through teaching and assessing, a school may have a strong draft of priority standards in place, we recommend leadership teams establish a review timeline every two to three years to ensure ongoing refinement.

In some schools, teachers may receive professional learning on the importance of prioritizing standards, followed by an expectation that they prioritize all the standards for a single course or content area by the end of the year. In year 2, teams will likely need to revisit the priority standards they identified and utilized in year 1 based on each team's ability to teach, assess, reassess, and communicate the highest-priority standards in the gradebook or report card within the given number of instructional days. Also in year 2, leadership might expect teams to identify priority standards for the remaining courses and content areas after teacher teams are more familiar with the process. In year 3, teacher teams are in a position to revise their priority standards based on their experience teaching, assessing, reassessing, and communicating them during a school year.

Common Pitfalls When Communicating Current Levels of Learning

In addition to the four criteria teams need to meet to communicate current levels of learning, secondary educators should be aware of several pitfalls to avoid. These pitfalls include the following.

- Failing to regularly communicate with parents and students about completion of practice assignments

- Failing to communicate with parents and students about the shift from entering assessment scores to entering standards in the gradebook

- Including too many standards or standards that are difficult to assess in the gradebook

The following sections describe these pitfalls and how you can avoid them.

Failing to Regularly Communicate With Parents and Students About Completion of Practice Assignments

Although standards-based grading repurposes homework as ungraded practice (see chapter 3, page 47), teachers may feel tempted to simply not communicate homework completion so that it does not distract from emphasizing learning standards in the electronic gradebook. However, teachers, parents, and students can all benefit from being able to visualize homework assignments and the rate at which a student is (or is not) completing them. To present both sets of information together, without confusing homework and standards, teachers can use non-numerical indicators, such as *collected* and *missing*, in a student information system. These indicators communicate to students and parents the number of assignments a student has completed. Figure 2.5 illustrates the use of these indicators. Recall that figure 2.2 (page 28) shows a sample gradebook that integrates both homework and standards.

Social Studies		
Date	**Activity**	**Status**
9/20	Worksheet 1.1	✓
9/25	Worksheet 1.2	✓
9/30	Worksheet 1.3	X
	Key: ✓ = Collected X = Missing L = Late Ab = Absent	

Figure 2.5: Communicating completion of practice assignments using non-numerical indicators.

Teachers can also communicate the completion of practice assignments by *zero weighting* the assignments in the gradebook. In figure 2.6, you can see a student completed three out of five practice assignments in week 2. Traditionally, this would be reported as three out of five points; however, homework is repurposed as ungraded practice in standards-based grading.

Mathematics		
Date	**Standard or Assignment**	**Assignments Completed* or Proficiency Level**
9/10	Week 1 practice assignments	5 of 5*
9/15	Solve problems involving estimation.	2
9/20	Week 2 practice assignments	3 of 5*
9/25	Understand place value.	1
	Key: 0 = No evidence of learning 1 = Minimal understanding 2 = Partial understanding 3 = Proficiency with standards 4 = Mastery of standards * = Does not count toward course grade	

Figure 2.6: Standards-based gradebook communicating completion of practice assignments as zero weight.

Failing to Communicate With Parents and Students About the Shift From Entering Assessment Scores to Entering Standards in the Gradebook

Research from Peters and Buckmiller (2014) suggests understanding how to read and interpret student performance in online standards-based gradebooks is a barrier for schools in the early phases of moving to standards-based grading. This makes it even more important that teachers and school leaders clearly communicate to parents and students the gradebook's new look and purpose. When making the transition to standards-based grading, consider offering tutorial videos and annotated visuals that effectively communicate any new electronic gradebook navigation steps. Hosting parent nights and orientation events can also give secondary schools an opportunity to illustrate visuals of the old and new gradebooks. For schools that haven't fully rolled out standards-based grading, but do have early-adopting individual teachers or teams adopting it, the implementation or leadership team (a concept we explore in chapter 5, page 103) should advise those teachers to draft a letter to parents or dedicate a significant portion of their class syllabus to these changes.

We further discuss how to communicate with parents about all standards-based grading principles in chapter 5. Also, see appendix B (page 155) for a sample parent-communication letter.

Including Too Many Standards or Standards That Are Difficult to Assess in the Gradebook

Teachers commonly feel tempted to slice (divide) standards too much when rewording them to be student and parent friendly. Sometimes teachers believe a single state standard is so complex it is not possible to adequately assess it on its own. So instead of prioritizing the standards into a manageable list, they break down one state or national standard into several individually assessable parts. By drilling down too far and including many fine-grained statements of learning in the gradebook, teachers risk creating an unmanageable number of items to assess and track in the gradebook. Instead, transferability with the standard is the goal. Ultimately, we want students to be very clear about what they are learning. Complicated or vague statements communicated in a gradebook do nothing to help students better understand their learning.

Teachers have two steps for determining if a standard is too narrow or thin. First, they sort student work based on the level of understanding of the standard (0–4). For example, the first pile should include student work with no or minimal understanding of the standard, the second pile should include student work with partial understanding, the third pile should include student work that shows proficiency with the standard, and the fourth pile should include student work that shows mastery of the standard.

If teacher teams can easily sort these examples of student work into three to four piles, the standard may have enough depth to score holistically using an integer scale as a guide. Conversely, if teams find it challenging to sort examples of student work into these four piles, the standard may be too thinly worded. Thin standards are hard to assess, lack clarity, and lead to confusion for both students and teachers, making it nearly impossible to sort the student work samples.

For example, a U.S. History standard in Iowa states, "Determine multiple and complex causes and effects of historical events in American history including, but not limited to, the Civil War, World War I and II, the Korean War and the Vietnam War" (SS-US.9-12.26; Iowa Core, n.d.). A teacher team from our school sliced the standard too thin when it narrowly focused on John F. Kennedy's assassination, using the student-friendly language, *Understands three reasons why John F. Kennedy's assassination was important to the United States' history*. The challenge with this JFK example is that, throughout history, there are innumerable factors for why an assassination might take place. The purpose of the standard is meant to help students understand the greater idea of political factors and influences. Simply focusing on three reasons for Kennedy's assassination for this example is not transferable to other examples of political factors and influences.

The second step in determining if a standard is too thin has teachers consider what the reassessment process might look like. Due to the way the John F. Kennedy example is written, it leaves no room to alter the standard's corresponding assessment question. It would require students to write again their understanding of three reasons he was assassinated. A more manageable standard with a similar theme might read, *Understands multiple reasons why political leaders have been assassinated and makes connections to current stories in mass media*. Using this standard, a history, civics, or current-events teacher can ask students to connect the events of John F. Kennedy's and any other political figure's assassinations with any events that may have recently taken place.

In summary, teachers must write standards in a way that permits them enough depth to assess student learning while simultaneously permitting student learning to transfer to other content areas, situations, or examples.

Assessment Tools for Your Journey

When educators desire to clarify change, they might create an innovation-configuration map. An *innovation-configuration map* describes the components of an innovation and the steps or activities to fully implement the innovation. This map helps educators plan implementation supports and self-reflect (Hall & Hord, 2015). The standards-based grading continua we use in this section and in subsequent chapters are examples of innovation-configuration maps describing how to implement standards-based grading in a secondary classroom.

Figure 2.7 (page 42) and figure 2.8 (page 44) show the standards-based grading continuum for the first principle—grades should communicate students' current levels of learning based on standards. Figure 2.7 is for individual teachers to fill out. Once each teacher has assessed him- or herself, the team should use figure 2.8 to assess itself. (See pages 136 and 142 for reproducible versions of these continua.) Departments, leadership teams, and entire schools may use the self-reported levels of implementation for each standards-based grading guideline to plan their next implementation supports.

After completing both the individual and team assessments, use the action-plan template in figure 2.9 (page 45) to write down your and your team's current levels of implementation and next steps. (See page 147 for a reproducible version of this action-plan template.)

Directions: As an individual, circle each criterion that aligns with your current level of implementation of the first standards-based grading principle—grades should communicate students' current levels of learning based on standards. Consider the evidence following the criteria as examples of artifacts you or other team members can provide or share with each other as well as other teams in your PLC. Note it is possible to circle criteria from multiple categories.

Getting Started	Implementing	Sustaining
Criteria: Numbers in the gradebook are based on assessment tasks.	**Criteria:** Some, but not all numbers in the gradebook are based on standards rather than assessment tasks.	**Criteria:** All numbers in the gradebook are based on standards rather than assessment tasks.
None of my standards are based on state, provincial, or national standards.	Most of my standards are based on state, provincial, or national standards.	All my standards are based on state, provincial, or national standards.
I have not yet taken the time to look at the number of standards I teach in each course to see if it is manageable to assess and record them all.	I have looked at the number of standards I assess and record in each course; however, I am not yet sure if my list is manageable.	I regularly review the number of standards I assess and record in each course, and I believe my list is manageable for the most part.
When I return an assessment to students, it usually includes one overall score.	When I return an assessment to students, it includes a score for each standard assessed.	When I return an assessment to students, it includes a score for each standard assessed, and I have rewritten these standards in a way that students and parents can understand.

Evidence: Gradebooks include assessment tasks such as homework, quizzes, tests, and projects.	**Evidence:** Gradebooks include a mix of assessment tasks such as homework, quizzes, tests, and projects, as well as number based upon standards. All numbers in the gradebook are based on standards.	**Evidence:** All numbers in the gradebook are based on standards.
Course standards are not yet documented or reviewed.	There is written or verbal articulation between course standards and state, provincial, or national standards.	There is written articulation between course standards and state, provincial, or national standards.
I am not aware of the number of standards I am assessing.	I have discomfort with the number of standards.	I am comfortable with the number of standards.
Completed student assessments indicate one overall score.	Completed student assessments indicate point-based scores for each standard.	Completed student assessments indicate numbers, such as 1–4, based on the level of learning for each standard (which are written in a parent- and student-friendly way).

Figure 2.7: Continuum for standards-based grading principle 1—individual assessment.

Directions: As a team, circle each criterion that aligns with your team's current level of implementation of the first standards-based grading principle—grades should communicate students' current levels of learning based on standards. Consider the evidence following the criteria as examples of artifacts your team members can provide or share with each other as well as other teams in your PLC. Note it is possible to circle criteria from multiple categories.

Getting Started	Implementing	Sustaining
Criteria: Our team has not yet identified priority standards for our courses or content areas.	**Criteria:** Our team has identified priority standards for some, but not all, of our courses or content areas.	**Criteria:** Our team has identified priority standards for all our courses or content areas. Each year, our team meets to consider revising the priority standards for our courses or content areas.
Evidence: The standards taught in a course or content area are dependent on individual teachers.	**Evidence:** Our team has a list of identified priority standards for one or several courses or content areas.	**Evidence:** Our team has a list of identified priority standards for each course or content area. Previous versions of priority standards and team minutes note the revision process used to review priority standards.

Figure 2.8: Continuum for standards-based grading principle 1—team assessment.

My current level on the continuum for the first standards-based grading principle—grades should communicate students' current levels of learning based on standards—is best described as (circle one):

Getting started   **Implementing**   **Sustaining**

Evidence I can provide to support my current level includes:

My next steps will be:

My team's current level on the continuum for the first standards-based grading principle—grades should communicate students' current levels of learning based on standards—is best described as (circle one):

Getting started   **Implementing**   **Sustaining**

Evidence my team can provide to support our current level includes:

Directions: Use the following table to plan your team's next steps.

Desired Level and Criteria: Where do we want to be?	**Action:** What do we need to do to move closer to sustaining on the standards-based grading continuum for this principle?	**Change:** What do we need to change or give up?	**Evidence of Success:** What products, policies, or procedures would demonstrate our desired criteria?

Figure 2.9: Action-plan template for standards-based grading principle 1.

CHAPTER 3

How Homework Serves as Ungraded Practice

In any middle or high school, ten minutes before the first bell rings, seasoned educators know they will find students sitting in the lunchroom or standing in the hallways discussing their weekend plans or adventures, ideas for prom dates, or predictions on the Friday-night football game. Intermixed, they'll find another familiar sight—students copying homework assignments! Notebook swaps, worksheet glances, and lab report summarizations are the norm. Secondary students are pressed each day to perform well on homework assignments or else fall behind in the point-accumulation game that takes place throughout the school year. Class rank and grade point averages are at stake. For students aiming for high achievement, a few incomplete assignments can be the difference between the 10th and 11th percentiles of the class. Conversely, for students not aiming to maximize achievement, homework is often an obstacle to be dodged.

It's no wonder that homework is a major source of angst, not only for students but teachers too (Paulu, 1998). As such, teachers often devise ways to reward students for completing their homework assignments, such as the following.

- "Turn in five consecutive homework assignments, and earn a free homework pass!"

- "Earn a B or better on the test, and homework is optional for the next chapter!"

- "Complete all of your homework on Monday through Thursday, and the weekend is homework free!"

Matt once told his students a daily mathematics assignment would be worth one hundred points, rather than its usual five points. The same students who always completed the homework also completed this assignment, while the usual suspects brushed it off.

All these strategies emphasize completing homework for the sake of earning points or the opportunity to skip future assignments. Both methods send the same subliminal message: "Homework is worth doing because points matter. Learning is optional." As Daniel H. Pink (2011) puts it, "We're bribing students into compliance instead of challenging them into engagement" (p. 174). In addition, grades only motivate students who are motivated by grades—and some students couldn't care less.

John Hattie's (2009) meta-analysis suggests feedback has a positive influence on student achievement when students know the learning goal and receive suggestions related to that desired state. Points and percentages themselves typically noted at the top of a homework assignment do not provide this level of feedback. In a typical classroom, teachers assign homework multiple times per week; therefore, it makes sense for teachers to maximize feedback opportunities through their homework assignment and collection routines. One such homework policy statement reads:

> *Teachers should provide students with multiple opportunities to practice standards independently through homework or other classwork; however, teachers should be consistent with classroom standards for the purpose of providing feedback.*

> *Practice assignments, including homework, should not be included as part of the final grade.*

This statement cuts to the core of homework's role in standards-based grading, which is to serve as practice and a mechanism for formative feedback, both of which increase learning. When homework points are tied to completion, as they typically are in a traditional point-based system, the emphasis is *doing* the work instead of *learning*.

We believe that when homework is formative and designed to provide feedback, students are more inclined to seek purposeful learning through practice rather than compliance. Indeed, the purpose of this chapter is to describe how you can repurpose homework as ungraded independent practice that provides supportive feedback, which is the second standards-based grading principle. In addition, this chapter explains how to connect this principle to your work within a PLC, describes common pitfalls to avoid, and provides a standards-based grading continuum and an action-plan template to help you assess your journey and determine next steps in implementing this grading principle.

Four Criteria for Implementing Homework as Ungraded Practice

Madeline Hunter's well-documented and seminal lesson-planning model includes an anticipatory set grabbing the class's attention, followed by some type of instructional input (such as lecture, small-group activities, or inquiry) working toward an overarching objective (Stallings, 1985). Later, the teacher models the skill, product, or process. The Hunter model ends with a check for understanding, guided practice, and finally, independent practice.

Stemming from this historical and frequently implemented lesson-planning model, *independent practice*, which parents and students alike commonly refer to as *homework*, is a time-honored tradition in secondary schools. (In this book, we use both terms interchangeably.) Students typically turn in homework assignments the following day, and teachers return the homework sometime after that with a score. Homework usually receives a point value for one of several reasons. Some teachers believe grading homework promotes accountability and improves an individual's level of responsibility (Vatterott, 2018). Other teachers believe grading homework places value on the task.

Why should teachers in a PLC change this practice and not assign homework a point value? Through its collaborative structure, teachers in a PLC value knowing when students have demonstrated learning. But because students often complete homework outside of class and potentially with the assistance of other adults or peers, it is not always the most reliable medium for determining students' current levels of learning. Students also need an opportunity to apply for themselves the concepts or ideas they are currently learning in class. Homework repurposed as independent practice affords students the opportunity to apply their learning and make mistakes in a safe environment that does not penalize their academic grade.

The following sections thoroughly describe the four criteria needed to implement homework as ungraded independent practice.

1. Homework should not be part of students' final grade.

2. Students should receive feedback on the majority of their homework.

3. Homework should be purposeful and connect to course and grade standards.

4. Teachers should regularly work with students who are struggling due to incomplete homework.

Homework Should Not Be Part of Students' Final Grade

As we touched on in chapter 2 (page 21), in a connected world, parents and students frequently have access to teachers' gradebooks in real time. Parents who wish to find out how well their students are doing simply log in weekly, daily, or sometimes hourly. Faculty handbooks often dictate the frequency with which teachers must update their electronic gradebooks and the deadlines they have to complete student report cards. It is also common that schools and teachers encourage students to access their grades electronically so the students can identify missing assignments or discrepancies between turned-in artifacts and the gradebook. Many online gradebooks enable users to set up automatic email or text message triggers when teachers enter new grades, when an assignment is missing, or if a student earns a less-than-desirable grade.

The problem is that all these historical and well-intentioned practices are a bit misleading. Parents and students have been trained to monitor task completion, points, and percentages, which they assume to be measures of learning. Points have become the currency of the classroom, and homework is both frequent and the easiest to document. At the same time, homework completion does not represent learning, and it simultaneously creates extra work for teachers to determine a number for the purpose of data entry on each individual assignment, regardless of its formative or summative purpose. With all these complicating factors, it begs the question: Why do educators continue to grade homework in a traditional grading system?

Cathy Vatterott (2011) suggests three reasons teachers continue to grade homework that, by this point in the chapter, should ring familiar. In teacher speak, the reasons are (1) "If I don't grade it, they won't do it," (2) "Hard work should be rewarded," and (3) "Homework grades help students who test poorly." After attending a mathematics teacher's conference, Matt started to think about some of these ideas about homework. No matter the point value assigned to a homework assignment, the same students seemed to be completing and not completing it each day, dispelling the first and second reasons. Similarly, he also noted that, while the points awarded for homework did help students who tested poorly, it did not ensure their success in future mathematics classes. This indicated to Matt the need for a significant classroom change related to grading homework.

Matt did not want to take students by surprise, so before he transitioned to ungraded homework assignments halfway through a semester, he sought to help his students understand the connections among homework, hard work, and success on assessments. He asked students to consider the reasons why they would or would not complete homework assignments based on various point values. A dialogue similar to the following ensued. We should note in this scenario that Matt had developed a positive rapport with the student, Chris. We do not recommend trying this approach without first establishing a positive relationship *in* the class.

> **Matt Townsley:** *I have been thinking a lot about homework lately. You know that each day, I currently grade your homework assignments based on effort and showing work and that you can earn up to three points per day. If I told you tomorrow's assignment was worth one point instead of three, how many of you would complete it?* (A few students raise their hands.)

> *Thank you. Now, if I told you the homework assignments in this class were worth zero points, how many of you would complete them?* (Even fewer students raise their hands.)

> *Rochelle, I noticed you raised your hand. Tell us, why would you continue to do the homework assignments if they weren't worth any points?*

> **Rochelle:** *My mom would kill me if I didn't do my homework!*

> **Matt Townsley:** *Thank you for your honesty. Chris, I noticed you did not raise your hand. Why wouldn't you do the homework assignments if they weren't worth any points?*

> **Chris:** *C'mon, Mr. T.! I'd be spending all of my free time playing the new Xbox games!*

> **Matt Townsley:** *Chris, I very much appreciate your honesty. However, if you did not do any of the homework, how well do you think you'd do on the next chapter test?*

> **Chris:** *Well, I think I'd probably fail it, Mr. T.; but I'd get really good at my new Xbox games.*

> **Matt Townsley:** *OK, Chris. That's enough. Chris, if you did not do any of the homework for the next chapter, how well do you think you'd do on that chapter test?*

> **Chris:** *I'd probably fail it too.*

> **Matt Townsley:** *Chris, how many tests do you think you'd fail before you'd realize that doing the homework is a good idea?*

Chris: I don't know . . . four or five maybe?

Matt Townsley: Thank you again for your honesty, Chris. Let's not wait four or five tests to figure out what we already know today. The purpose of homework in this class is practice and for you to receive feedback. I don't think it is fair to penalize you for practicing poorly; however, I believe it is important for you to practice. I will do my best to assign practice problems only when needed. All of the answers will be available right here on the wall, in the back of the book, or on my website so that you can access them from home or at the library.

This approach is not a magic bullet for motivating students to complete ungraded homework, but it can serve as a memorable milestone for future conversations. If or when a student does not turn in a practice assignment, the teacher can quickly refer to this milestone as a reminder of the purpose of practice assignments and the repercussions of not completing them (failing to demonstrate an understanding of concepts and therefore earning a poor grade on the summative assessment).

Our experience tells us that when secondary schools implement homework as ungraded practice in a standards-based grading system, teachers should expect a dip in homework completion. Some students will take the liberty of not completing homework because it is no longer assigned a point value. Our experience in the Solon Community School District suggests that following this initial dip, many teachers strongly emphasize the practice purpose behind homework. As a result, we find that many students come to realize homework completion is ultimately valuable in their learning experience as they come to associate their homework with their ability to achieve clear learning standards. Perhaps most importantly, both teachers and students become much more focused on the quantity of homework assigned. Only the unique problems, exercises, and activities needed to help individual students need to be assigned. In time, homework completion rates at our secondary schools rebounded to nearly the same as before our standards-based grading implementation. Figure 3.1 depicts the typical implementation dip and ensuring rebound.

In our experiences, teachers often find themselves hiding behind points. Rather than confronting students who are not turning in homework assignments, they abide by a previously communicated and often zero-tolerance homework policy. When students do not complete homework, they say, "Late homework will not be accepted," and enter a zero into the gradebook. Teachers continue to enact this punishment on many of the same students year after year without it changing the students' behavior. The result is seniors in high schools across the United States receiving zeros each day

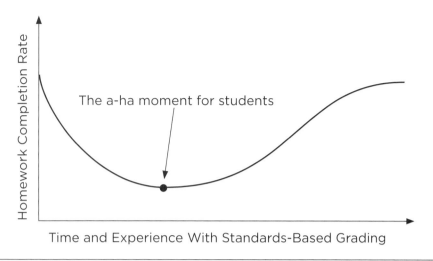

Figure 3.1: Completion curve when implementing ungraded homework.

for the fourth year in a row, a cause of emotional distress and students dropping out of school (Reeves, 2004). In the meantime, some students are unnecessarily completing homework assignments beneath their proficiency level to chase points even though they can already demonstrate a thorough understanding of the homework exercises' concepts.

All the while, teachers avoid confronting the reality that unique circumstances surround individual students' inability to complete homework. Annabelle struggles to find time to complete the assignments because she is working evening shifts at the local convenience store in order to put food on the table for her family. Tom finds himself babysitting his younger sister nearly every night while his father and his girlfriend scream so loud that the whole floor of their apartment complex can often hear them. Jemele feels so much pressure to make the honor roll that she puts off studying for her test in biology (a class she struggles to understand) so she can complete mathematics homework problems she has already mastered because they are worth 40 percent of her grade.

In *Classroom Instruction That Works*, a book loaded with research-based strategies for increasing student achievement, Ceri B. Dean, Elizabeth Ross Hubbell, Howard Pitler, and Bj Stone (2012) summarize, "Providing feedback (rather than grades) on homework can encourage students to take risks and show teachers aspects of their conceptual understanding that they might not have revealed on a graded assignment" (p. 108).

We'll explore further the role of feedback in the next section, but it's important to note that ungraded homework has three other benefits: when homework does not directly influence a student's final grade, it (1) frees up teachers to focus on other tasks, (2) allows teachers to foster conversations with students about the root cause of their lack of practice, and (3) permits teachers to more openly individualize assignments for students. Think of the preceding examples of Annabelle, Tom, and Jemele and how these benefits enable teachers to adapt homework to better support each student's unique needs. Some students may need to work through ten problems out of class, others may need just three problems, and still others may not need to practice anything at all due to their positive demonstrations of learning during classroom checks for understanding.

Although it's a valid concern that differentiating work in this way can feel punitive for students receiving more work to do, we believe that when teachers proactively clarify to students that the intent is to personalize learning, similar to the way a personal trainer customizes a weight-lifting workout, that students understand this. Further, those who need a challenge should receive opportunities for extension (PLC critical question 4) just as those who may still be struggling should receive appropriate practice tasks. Regardless of the homework assignment, all students should receive feedback on their work.

Students Should Receive Feedback on the Majority of Their Homework

Although we recommend repurposing homework as ungraded practice, do not interpret this as support for eliminating homework. Because homework offers teachers the opportunity to formatively assess students and provide feedback to support learning, whether done in class or at home, this independent practice is critical to student learning and the standards-based grading school. In fact, a meta-analysis suggests homework has a higher effect size in upper grades when compared to elementary (Baş, Şenturk, & Ciğerci, 2017). In other words, as grade levels increase, so does homework's positive influence on student learning outcomes. This does not mean all homework is created equal. Instead, teachers should use independent practice assignments based on the proficiency and skills of individual students.

Based on in-class activities and previous checks for understanding, a secondary teacher may determine the specific homework activities needed to provide just-in-time feedback for students. Social psychologist and published expert on homework's effectiveness Harris Cooper (1989) also reminds teachers that they should minimize their grading of homework. It is important that teachers not confuse grading homework with giving students feedback on it. In this section, we explore two examples of supportive and helpful feedback based on homework performance.

As a means to give students the feedback they most needed, Matt adopted a *traffic light* approach to homework and practice assignments. When he was a high school mathematics teacher, he provided all the answers to practice problems the same day he assigned them. Rather than having students wait twenty-four hours to check their understanding, he encouraged them to immediately check their answers against those posted on the board. He frequently posted the same answers on the class website so students could check them at home or from the local library.

The next day, Matt invited students to check any remaining answers on their papers against those on the board. He also included a Questions box on the board where students could write the numbers of problems they still had questions about. He went over these solutions as a whole class before asking students to *traffic light* their papers, labeling the papers with the color that represented their level of understanding. A red label indicated they were very unsure of their work, a yellow label indicated they had partial understanding, and a green label communicated that they were confident they understood the concepts practiced on the assignment. This approach has additional benefits beyond engaging students in self-assessment. By specifically allowing students to self-evaluate their comfort level with learning material, teachers can target their feedback to each student accordingly. As Susan M. Brookhart (2008) puts it, "Feedback says to the student, 'Somebody cared enough about my work to read it and think about it!'" (p. 1).

When this traffic light practice became embedded in their course, students started to write notes to Matt along with their lights. Through this process, Matt could take time to write feedback to the students that helped them with their specific struggles or offered pathways to extend learning for those showing mastery, and because of this, the students shared they were more likely to carefully read the feedback written on these papers than on previous assignments. We believe this written dialogue between teacher and student facilitates a *we're in this together* mentality. It shows students that their teacher cares about them and their learning.

As a second example of using homework as a vehicle for feedback, at Solon High School, English teacher Ivy Nielsen regularly assigns comprehension questions for students to complete while reading portions of *The Tragedy of Romeo and Juliet* (Shakespeare, 1935). She goes over answers as a whole group the following day and uses the students' responses to ask follow-up questions that rate higher on Bloom's taxonomy revised (Anderson & Krathwohl, 2001). In this context, checking homework serves a multifaceted purpose—checking for comprehension *and* extending comprehension beyond rote recall.

By keeping homework ungraded and using it to support and extend learning through feedback, teachers can more effectively keep their students' focus on gaining skills rather than accumulating points.

Homework Should Be Purposeful and Connect to Course and Grade Standards

Cathy Vatterott (2010) suggests five characteristics of effective homework: it (1) shows a clear purpose, (2) efficiently demonstrates student learning, (3) promotes ownership, (4) instills competence without adult assistance, and (5) assigns enjoyable tasks. The first characteristic, *shows a clear purpose*, is the one that standards-based grading advocates home in on. When teachers do not have a clear purpose for homework in mind, their assignments may seem like busywork. For example, a mathematics instructor who does not connect course or grade standards to practice may regularly assign all students to complete the same set of problems, such as *even-numbered problems from 2 to 30*, regardless of whether they align with the day's concepts or the exercise's connections to the intended learning targets.

When teachers do have a clear purpose for homework in mind, it helps students see the nexus between practice and the standards. For example, when a teacher has a clear purpose for homework, he or she might provide students with a weekly assignment organizer. In this organizer, students see the practice problems assigned as well as the standards to which each exercise set aligns. Figure 3.2 illustrates an example of a mathematics teacher's weekly assignments connected with standards.

As another example, a family and consumer sciences teacher writes the learning target, *Demonstrate menu-planning principles and techniques*, on the board. During the class period, students critique area restaurant menus using a teacher-provided rubric. The class homework assignment is to search the internet for a menu of a well-rated restaurant in a neighboring county. Students must also write a brief paragraph identifying menu-planning principles the owner or head chef may have used or failed to use. In turn, students make a clear connection between their homework assignment and the target written on the board.

As a final example, a sixth-grade teacher might assign a certain number of pages for reading each night to help students practice their reading comprehension. Students can track how many books they complete, and the teacher can provide incentives for reading. For instance, instead of using points to incentivize reading, a teacher may choose to provide several healthy snack options once the class has met an agreed-on number of cumulative pages. Another incentive might include celebrating William

Weekly Assignments for Geometry		
Day	**Homework or practice assignment**	**Connection to class standards**
Monday	Worksheet 8.5	Derive the equation of a circle.
Tuesday	p. 455 (problems 1–5, 8, 14–24 [evens], 28)	Derive the equation of a circle.
Wednesday	Worksheet 8.6	Derive the equation of a parabola.
Thursday	Review worksheet	Derive the equation of a circle (worksheet questions 1–4). Derive the equation of a parabola (worksheet questions 5–8).
Friday	None (quiz)	Derive the equation of a circle. Derive the equation of a parabola.

Figure 3.2: Organizer to connect homework assignments to learning standards.

Shakespeare's birthday when enough students have read a specific number of pages from classical literature. Both of these examples are purposeful in directing students to practice intended course standards related to reading comprehension while keeping the emphasis on learning rather than points. They are also beneficial for the teacher because he or she can monitor the students' reading level and provide feedback throughout the year. Further, teachers can differentiate readings based on students' proficiency, allowing them to select books that fit their reading level or those that most interest them.

We describe a more formal and detailed process for writing a team-developed homework purpose statement in this chapter's PLC Connection section (page 59).

Teachers Should Regularly Work With Students Who Are Struggling Due to Incomplete Homework

As we established in Homework Should Not Be Part of Students' Final Grade (page 50), in traditional grading systems, teachers can punish students for not completing homework by reducing their points. For students who chronically fail to complete homework, this punishment often carries on, year over year, without changing the students' behavior. Conversely, some students are completing unnecessary home-work assignments to chase points when they can already demonstrate a thorough understanding of the homework exercises' concepts. Although this strategy of using grades as punishment is common, its long-term effectiveness for improving learning outcomes for struggling students is questionable at best (Guskey, 2015a). We know that teachers usually do not consciously decide to hide behind points, but it happens. Teachers must be mindful about confronting the reality of each student rather than maintain this punishment. PLC culture demands that teachers have an answer to the question of what to do when students do not learn and how to extend learning for students that achieve high proficiency. In this section, we focus on the former.

When teachers who successfully use standards-based grading note a lack of home-work completion through the online gradebook, they are not afraid to communicate with students and parents about this trend via a quick phone call or email. The goal is not to punish but to work toward effective solutions when homework completion issues arise. One example is creating individualized student homework contracts to improve student motivation to complete homework assignments. Students agree to complete practice assignments and, in return, receive points they can cash in for rewards, such as sitting in a seat of their choice during class or leaving class for lunch one minute early. As a teacher, Matt also used the last five minutes of class for students to begin working on their practice assignments. When a student successfully showed that he or she understood a concept on one of the early mathematics problems, he often permitted him or her to skip later problems related to the same concept. This motivated students to successfully complete as many practice problems as possible during class so they could have other practice problems removed from their individ-ualized evening assignment.

When a school begins to function as a true PLC, teachers direct, rather than invite, students to receive additional help (Buffum, Mattos, & Malone, 2018; DuFour et al., 2016). Because PLCs strive to ensure learning for *all* students, interventions for students who have not yet demonstrated an understanding of the course standards become an important pillar of the school's work. While directing students to inter-ventions comes naturally at elementary, secondary students are less likely to volunteer their time outside of class to seek extra help or to finish their incomplete practice assignments (Buffum et al., 2012). As such, teachers and teacher teams must be proactive in directing students to receive additional help.

This is why teachers at Solon High School have taken a different approach to home-work. Each week, classroom teachers refer students to the office who are struggling academically due to incomplete homework. The office staff have an intervention team that is assigned to look at all teacher referrals. This team then divides the students based on the teachers' requests and the students' grades during that week. If teachers requested an intervention for a specific learning target, the students are assigned (during homeroom time) to the teacher that requested him or her. If the students are struggling simply because they are not doing the homework or practice, they are required to attend a structured study hall with the principal during this homeroom time. This also allows the principal an opportunity to talk to students about the importance of practice during the learning process. Because a PLC works toward ensuring all students learn at high levels, it only makes sense that the penalty for not doing the work is spending time doing the work.

As you reflect on this, consider Cardinal High School in Eldon, Iowa, which implemented a similar system in its school that they called *Ketchup Solution*. As a result of penalizing students for not completing their work by requiring them to spend time doing the work, class failures reduced 96 percent (Reeves, 2012).

Teacher collaboration is the key to student success in both of these approaches. For the initially disorganized student, teachers had to teach them organization. Other teachers sacrificially suggested the assignments for their courses were a second priority when compared to the more immediate assignments of a colleague. With student success as the focus, collaborative teams can proactively assist students who are struggling due to incomplete homework.

PLC Connection

Repurposing homework as ungraded practice is a standards-based grading principle best implemented by teams of teachers working collaboratively. Although individual teachers can accomplish a number of the aforementioned criteria, teams of teachers functioning within a schoolwide or districtwide PLC are best equipped to repurpose homework as ungraded practice in a way that sends a consistent message to students and parents. Even if you have individual teachers who adamantly want to stick to having graded homework, here's why it's important for treating homework as ungraded practice to be a schoolwide endeavor: when one teacher assigns homework a point value and gives it a weight of 10 percent of the final grade while another teacher does not assign any point value to homework, students and parents receive mixed messages about the value and importance of homework.

Individual teachers often make decisions about the prioritization and purpose of homework with the best intentions, but teams of teachers are better positioned to make these decisions using a unified homework purpose statement. This unified purpose ensures all students have an equitable learning environment regardless of the classroom. Once unified in their purpose of homework, teacher teams can discuss and provide enhanced supports to students who are not currently completing the homework. The goal of this section is to provide teacher teams with practical steps for creating a homework purpose statement as well as suggest a realistic timeline for accomplishing this important work.

The process of coming to a schoolwide consensus on a homework purpose statement may require considerable discussion and work across collaborative teams. At Solon High School, we considered several drafts over the course of an entire school year before building a consensus. When teacher teams meet to develop a team or schoolwide homework purpose statement that repurposes homework as ungraded practice, they should consider the first two critical questions of a PLC (DuFour et al., 2016)—What is it we want our students to learn? and How will we know when each student has learned it? When a teacher team uses standards-based grading, team members should assign all homework with the first critical question in mind such that it permits students to practice the standards the team intends for them to learn.

As part of developing a homework purpose statement, teams should clearly state their philosophy and intentions related to homework completion. Giving consideration to previous homework practices may be helpful for teams to understand their collective approach from a traditional view of homework's purpose to a mindset rooted in standards-based grading practices.

Homework must still be evaluated and even scored, but in the event teachers in a standards-based grading system consider accuracy in scoring a homework assignment, they should not record this in the gradebook, because the intent of the assignment is to practice rather than to demonstrate mastery. For example, rather than recording a number in the gradebook, a history teacher might choose to write several sentences of feedback on a paragraph students submitted reflecting upon the causes of the Civil War in the United States. Yet, it is important in this scenario for the teacher to document this assignment as collected and completed on time in the electronic gradebook. Refer to figure 2.5 (page 38) for an example of the gradebook communicating this change in practice.

Due to its formative nature, teachers should not solely use homework tasks to determine how they will know if each student has learned the material. Instead, homework, common formative assessments, and other checks for understanding serve as a dipstick informing the teacher's next instructional actions. Teachers then use the results from summative assessments to communicate student learning in the gradebook relative to standards. (Refer to chapter 2, page 21, for additional information on communicating current levels of learning in the gradebook.) However, when considering the third PLC critical question—How will we respond when some students do not learn?—teams will benefit from looking at students' historical homework completion.

Consider a student who has completed all the homework assignments but has not yet learned the intended standard. The teachers assigned to this student will likely respond by creating one or more skill-based interventions. This is in contrast to a student who regularly does not complete homework assignments *and* has not yet learned the standard. The teachers assigned to that student will likely respond by creating a will-based intervention.

With this context in mind, teams should consider their responses to the questions in figure 3.3. We'll take a more thorough look at answering each question next.

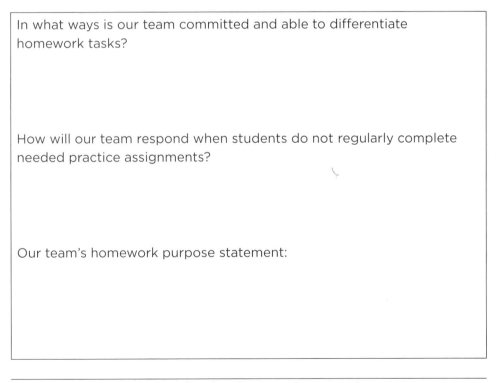

In what ways is our team committed and able to differentiate homework tasks?

How will our team respond when students do not regularly complete needed practice assignments?

Our team's homework purpose statement:

Figure 3.3: Team template for developing a homework purpose statement.

Visit go.SolutionTree.com/PLCbooks for a free reproducible version of this figure.

Differentiating homework can be a strong motivator for students when it comes to completion rates. Teachers can differentiate homework by difficulty or by the amount of work (Vatterott, 2018). For example, a student with below-grade-level reading ability may need a different article to read for a social studies homework assignment than his or her peers do. Similarly, students who have already demonstrated their understanding of solving algebraic equations may receive a more difficult or challenging problem set in their homework assignment than their classmates. When considering the amount of work in a homework assignment, teachers might differentiate homework based on students' ability and persistence in completing such work. Cathy Vatterott (2018) reminds teachers that assigning less work often increases student motivation, especially for students who may need additional time and support.

Although many strategies increase student motivation, there is no silver bullet that ensures all students will complete every single homework assignment. Despite a team's best efforts, some students will not complete the homework assignments designed to practice standards. To address this, teams in a PLC ask what they will do when some students do not learn, which may include students who have not yet demonstrated understanding stemming from their incomplete homework assignments. Effective schools establish a schoolwide system of interventions for students who consistently struggle to complete homework, or a team of teachers may establish its own collective response for when students do not complete homework.

One starting point for collaborative teams may be to list all students in their classes who are currently struggling to consistently complete homework assignments, including the duration and frequency of the missing work. Once the team has a list of names, each student's teacher should identify potential causes for these missing assignments, a task that may require consulting teachers on other departmental teams (depending on team structure). Common causes include extended absences, a current crisis or challenge the student is experiencing at home, or a simple lack of organizational or time-management skills. Figure 3.4 provides teams of teachers with a template for identifying students and potential causes for consistent struggles to complete homework assignments. After identifying each student and the potential reason for his or her struggles, teacher teams should prescribe a potential intervention. These interventions should initially be led by collaborative teacher teams and, if difficulties persist, a schoolwide intervention team (Buffum et al., 2018).

Student's name	Number of missing assignments	Last date the student turned in a homework assignment	Possible cause or causes for the missing work	Intervention to consider

Figure 3.4: Template for identifying the cause of incomplete homework.

*Visit **go.SolutionTree.com/PLCbooks** for a free reproducible version of this figure.*

Once teams have evaluated the cause (or causes) for missing homework, the final step is to write a team-developed homework purpose statement. The following is a sample homework purpose statement.

> *The purpose of homework on our team is to allow students to practice and make mistakes through independent and group work. At least once per week, we will differentiate homework assignments for students (through difficulty and amount), striving to balance the individual needs of our students with our ability to modify the district-provided curriculum materials. Every Tuesday, students who have not completed at least two homework assignments during the week will be assigned to Mrs. Jones's room during lunch for homework intervention. We will provide feedback on practice assignments, but we will not include them as part of the final academic grade.*

Following the completion of a team-developed homework purpose statement, teacher teams in a PLC should ensure they have a unified approach to students who struggle with homework completion by establishing skill- and will-based interventions (see page 27). During team collaboration time, teams should frequently discuss the effectiveness of their process for supporting students who are not regularly completing homework. For example, using the sample homework purpose statement on this page, teacher teams may discover that students who are assigned to Mrs. Jones's homework intervention time multiple times per month need an even more intensive homework completion intervention, something a team of teachers should create.

Because teachers in a PLC are committed to continuous improvement and collective inquiry into best practice (DuFour et al., 2008), this ongoing and systematic response to students' homework completion will inevitably be a challenging yet necessary process.

Common Pitfalls When Using Homework as Ungraded Practice

In addition to the four criteria needed to repurpose homework as ungraded practice, secondary educators should be aware of the following pitfalls to avoid.

- Entering students' first attempt at homework into the gradebook and then overwriting it as students improve
- Not recording homework completion
- Failing to use homework to identify the need for intervention

The following sections describe these pitfalls and how you can avoid them.

Entering Students' First Attempt at Homework Into the Gradebook and Then Overwriting It as Students Improve

Some teachers advocate using homework assignments as part of the final grade as long as the most recent assignment or assessment score is used. For example, an algebra teacher enters a failing grade for a student whose first homework attempt demonstrates he or she does not yet understand how to graph linear equations in slope-intercept form. At this early point in time, we would not expect all algebra students to understand slope-intercept form because they have only received one class period of instruction. Later, the teacher replaces the score after the student improves his or her understanding of this concept on the end-of-chapter review assignment, following several more days of teaching, reteaching, and review.

The problem with this approach of assigning point values to attempts at learning following very little classroom instruction is that it can create a kindergarten effect, in which many students earn low grades at an early phase in the learning cycle yet demonstrate understanding of the learning outcomes by the end of the year. Parents and students who frequently check their grades via electronic gradebooks may be alarmed to see lower than desired grades and may ask premature questions to the teacher about the student's lack of academic success.

Because the purpose of homework is for students to practice, we advocate it should not count at all toward the final grade. Ungraded homework affords students the important opportunity to make mistakes while practicing independently. It also gives teachers an important opportunity to share and receive feedback. Neither mistakes with homework nor teacher feedback on that homework need to be recorded in the gradebook in a way that influences the final academic grade.

Not Recording Homework Completion

When teachers do not count homework and independent practice assignments toward the final grade, they may be tempted to simply not communicate with students at all about what work they've completed. In this scenario, teachers mistakenly make the assumption that since homework is not graded, it doesn't need to be reported. We must make an important note here: *homework completion and practicing learning are essential to student learning.* By recording completion, teachers can communicate this important practice of learning to parents and students. In addition, recording completion communicates to parents the frequency in which their children are practicing the standards.

Teachers can overcome this pitfall if they use *collected* and *missing* indicators in a student information system, which communicate to students and parents the number of assignments a student has completed. It is important that a teacher not only record homework completion but also communicate to parents and students *how* he or she records that completion. Solon High School teacher Ken Beck clearly relays his intent to record homework completion in his chemistry course syllabus: "Homework will be tracked in the grading book. It will not be worth anything toward your grade, but it will be something that is charted" (personal communication, September 9, 2013).

Failing to Use Homework to Identify the Need for Intervention

Formative assessment, sometimes called *checking for understanding*, is the most important teacher action in standards-based grading. Students' results on formative assessments help guide a teacher's instruction. Often, teachers overlook homework as a tool for formative assessment by failing to recognize the wealth of information homework offers for teachers to glean insight into students' learning. What errors are occurring with student work? What misconceptions are present in homework answers? What are a student's strengths or weaknesses related to the standards? These are data, and these data highlight ways that homework can help guide teachers and collaborative teacher teams.

Further, when mistakes recur, it signals to the teacher the need for an intervention. Homework can be the most timely cue that a student will benefit from an intervention. When teachers only rely on more formal checks for understanding, such as weekly quizzes, they may be several days late in seeing a student's conceptual misnomer. Compared to a weekly quiz, daily homework or independent practice provides five opportunities during the week to offer clues to a student's level of proficiency. Similarly, if a collaborative team waits until the summative assessment, it may be too late to organize a timely intervention for the student. Remember, collaborative teams in a PLC seek to respond promptly when students are not yet learning (Buffum et al., 2018), and homework is an opportune means for gathering the necessary information to inform these decisions.

Assessment Tools for Your Journey

The major purpose of this chapter is to describe how to repurpose homework as ungraded practice, which is the second standards-based grading principle. Figure 3.5 and figure 3.6 (page 69) show the standards-based grading continuum for this principle. Figure 3.5 is for individual teachers to fill out. Once each teacher has assessed him- or herself, the team should use figure 3.6 to assess itself. (See pages 138 and 143 for reproducible versions of these continua.) Departments, leadership teams, and entire schools may use the self-reported levels of implementation for each standards-based grading guideline to plan their next implementation supports.

After completing both the individual and team assessments, use the action-plan template in figure 3.7 (page 70) to write down your and your team's current levels of implementation and next steps. (See page 149 for a reproducible version of this action-plan template.)

Directions: As an individual, circle each criterion that aligns with your current level of implementation of the second standards-based grading principle—homework should serve as ungraded practice. Consider the evidence following the criteria as examples of artifacts you or other team members can provide or share with each other as well as other teams in your PLC. Note it is possible to circle criteria from multiple categories.

Getting Started	Implementing	Sustaining
Criteria: Homework and independent practice are part of my students' final grade.	**Criteria:** Homework and practice assignments are not part of my students' final grade. Some students are able to articulate the role of homework and independent practice in my classes.	**Criteria:** Homework and practice assignments are not part of my students' final grade. Most students are able to articulate the role of homework and independent practice in my classes.
I give little feedback to my students.		
My homework and independent practice assignments do not have a clear connection to course standards.	My students receive feedback on some, but not all, of my homework and independent practice.	My students receive feedback on most of my homework and independent practice.
I do not use homework and independent practice to guide instruction.	Some, but not all, of my homework and independent practice assignments are purposeful and have a clear connection to course standards.	I can articulate the connection between all my homework and practice assignments and course standards as well as the purpose of each independent practice assignment.
	I occasionally address students who are not consistently completing homework and independent practice.	I regularly address students who are not consistently completing their homework and practice assignments, and I initiate contact with parents when a student is not completing the homework and independent practice.
	I sometimes use the results of homework and independent practice to guide instruction or provide interventions.	

Figure 3.5: Continuum for standards-based grading principle 2—individual assessment.

continued ▶

		I regularly use the results of homework and independent practice to guide instruction or provide interventions.
Evidence: My gradebook indicates homework and independent practice are part of students' final grade. My gradebook indicates that most students are not doing the homework and independent practice.	**Evidence:** Lesson plans indicate feedback opportunities (teacher, peer, textbook, online, and so on) for some homework and independent practice. I have examples of conversations with students who are not consistently completing homework and independent practice. My gradebook indicates that some students are completing homework and independent practice.	**Evidence:** Lesson plans indicate feedback opportunities (teacher, peer, textbook, online, and so on) for most homework and independent practice. I have a documented protocol I use to address students who are not consistently completing independent practice. I have multiple examples of conversations with students who are not consistently completing homework and independent practice. My gradebook indicates that the majority of students are completing homework and independent practice.

Directions: As a team, circle each criterion that aligns with your team's current level of implementation of the second standards-based grading principle—homework should serve as ungraded practice. Consider the evidence following the criteria as examples of artifacts your team members can provide or share with each other as well as other teams in your PLC. Note it is possible to circle criteria from multiple categories.

Getting Started	Implementing	Sustaining
Criteria: Teachers on our team have not created a homework purpose statement.	**Criteria:** Some, but not all, of the teachers on our team have created a homework purpose statement.	**Criteria:** Our team has a unified homework purpose statement based on two homework questions.
Evidence: No homework purpose statements exist.	**Evidence:** Individual homework purpose statements on the team differ significantly from one another.	**Evidence:** The team has a single team-developed homework purpose statement that communicates the purpose of homework as practice, the ways the team is committed to differentiating homework tasks, and how the team will respond when students do not regularly complete their practice assignments, and it identifies students needing intervention.

Figure 3.6: Continuum for standards-based grading principle 2—team assessment.

My current level on the continuum for the second standards-based grading principle—homework should serve as ungraded practice—is best described as (circle one):

Getting started   **Implementing**   **Sustaining**

Evidence I can provide to support my current level includes:

My next steps will be:

My team's current level on the continuum for the second standards-based grading principle—homework should serve as ungraded practice—is best described as (circle one):

Getting started   **Implementing**   **Sustaining**

Evidence my team can provide to support our current level includes:

Directions: Use the following table to plan your team's next steps.

Desired Level and Criteria: Where do we want to be?	**Action:** What do we need to do to move closer to sustaining on the standards-based grading continuum for this principle?	**Change:** What do we need to change or give up?	**Evidence of Success:** What products, policies, or procedures would demonstrate our desired criteria?

Figure 3.7: Action-plan template for standards-based grading principle 2.

CHAPTER 4

How to Provide Students With Multiple Opportunities to Demonstrate Their Learning

Because students learn differently and at varying rates, students who do not demonstrate understanding by a teacher-determined date should be allowed to demonstrate understanding at a later date. "Classroom assessments and grading should focus on how well—not on when—the student mastered the designated knowledge and skill" (McTighe & O'Connor, 2005, p. 17). This aligns with the second critical question of a PLC, How will we know when each student has learned it?

The need to understand when students have learned is why teacher teams in a PLC must develop a system that provides students with multiple opportunities to demonstrate their understanding. Retakes and revisions make student learning the *constant* in the classroom, not the *variable*, which is a key responsibility schools assume when adopting the PLC process (DuFour, DuFour, Eaker, & Karhanek, 2010). Furthermore, allowing students multiple opportunities helps teachers maximize the potential that students will master the essential standards for a course. In the article "Redos and Retakes Done Right," educational consultant Rick Wormeli (2011) writes:

> The goal is that *all* students learn the content, not just the ones who can learn on the uniform timeline. Curriculum goals don't require that every individual reaches the same level of proficiency on the same day, only that every student achieves the goal. (p. 22)

Allowing students multiple opportunities will most likely be met with criticism from skeptics. Some might say, "This doesn't prepare kids for real life!" while others might voice the concern, "We, as adults, don't get do-overs or retakes!" Those statements are

71

not accurate and do not reflect the learning process of adults or students. Wormeli (2011) continues:

> The teacher who claims to be preparing students for the working world by disallowing all redos forgets that adult professionals actually flourish through redos, retakes, and do-overs. Surgeons practice on cadavers before doing surgeries on live patients. Architects redesign building plans until they meet all the specifications listed. Pilots rehearse landings and takeoffs hundreds of times in simulators and in solo flights before flying with real passengers. Lawyers practice debate and analysis of arguments before litigating real cases. Teachers become much more competent and effective by teaching the same content multiple times, reflecting on what worked and what didn't work each time. . . . The best preparation for the world beyond school is to learn essential content and skills well. (p. 24)

In addition, skepticism of retakes runs contrary to one of the big ideas of a PLC, ensuring that all students learn (DuFour et al., 2016). Teams of teachers in a PLC are committed to a results orientation, in which achieving positive outcomes from students determines teachers' actions, rather than feeling comfortable when only some students succeed.

Through the process of giving students multiple opportunities to demonstrate their understanding, you can change the way your students think about learning in the classroom. You can help them understand that answers and solutions might not come on the first try and that new learning takes place over time, not by arbitrary deadlines.

This chapter describes how to provide students with multiple opportunities to demonstrate their learning, which is the third standards-based grading principle. In addition, it explains how to connect this principle to your work within a PLC, describes common pitfalls to avoid, and provides a standards-based grading continuum and an action-plan template to help you assess your journey and determine next steps in implementing this grading principle.

Six Criteria for Giving Students Multiple Opportunities to Demonstrate Their Learning

Perhaps a well-intentioned member of your PLC is hesitant to embrace the idea of providing students with multiple opportunities to demonstrate their learning. After all, he or she says, "There aren't redos in real life." Even after considering similar scenarios, such as how high school students are allowed to take the ACT and SAT tests multiple times, and driving tests are not a fail-once-and-you're-done type of exam, the idea of allowing students to provide further evidence of their learning after the whole-class assessment can seem soft in the eyes of some educators. Although we vehemently disagree with this perspective, there are situations in which we agree that a memorize-it-for-the-test approach is not well situated for learning.

For example, if students do not have to complete a cognitive task between consecutive attempts, and if the assessment prompts remain the same, then a system for retakes is unlikely to prove successful. Educational researcher Dylan Wiliam (2016) writes that schools allowing students to revise poor work and resubmit it for a higher grade may be detrimental to learning in the long run if students do not take an active role in the process. However, this sort of points-chasing event is not the intent of standards-based grading, and it does not align with a PLC's laser-like focus on learning.

The purpose of multiple opportunities for students to demonstrate learning is to use those opportunities to further that learning. Teachers adept at assessment *for* learning, sometimes called formative assessment, understand that you can't just take the first attempt at learning and consider that to be evidence of a student's overall understanding of that standard. Multiple measures, including early misconceptions, help better craft the overall understanding of students' knowledge. These teachers also know students should be involved in demonstrating their learning via multiple attempts, and, in between those attempts, they should have opportunities for self-assessment. This is why our experience suggests teachers should clearly articulate meaningful prerequisite steps before allowing a reassessment to take place while permitting students to have a voice in parts of the process. The following sections describe the six criteria needed to provide students with multiple opportunities to demonstrate their understanding.

1. Teachers should give individual students additional standards-based opportunities to demonstrate understanding.

2. Students should have a voice in how relearning takes place.

3. Teachers should have multiple ways of assessing the same standard for different students.

4. Teachers should communicate information related to reteaching and reassessment to parents.

5. Reassessment opportunities should be both teacher- and student-initiated.

6. Teachers should build in classroom time for reteaching before students reassess.

Teachers Should Give Individual Students Additional Standards-Based Opportunities to Demonstrate Understanding

Teachers should provide individual students with additional opportunities to demonstrate understanding after the final regularly scheduled whole-group assessment for that particular standard. In his theory of mastery learning, Benjamin Bloom prescribes that students differ in the amount of time it takes to learn, which is separate from their ability to learn (as cited in Guskey, 2015a). Because secondary teachers typically group learning into units of study, they often expect students to complete or submit the summative assessment on the same date at the end of the unit. If some students need additional time to demonstrate understanding while other students have already met proficiency, this places the teacher in a dilemma of whether or how to move on to the next unit without leaving these students behind.

One strategy standards-based grading offers to overcome this quandary is to give individual students additional standards-based opportunities to demonstrate understanding following the regularly scheduled whole-group assessment. This approach requires teachers to carefully plan the prerequisite criteria, time, and place for providing these additional opportunities. In a secondary school, this can take place during class, in study hall, in homeroom, or outside regular school hours. For example, Solon High School mathematics teacher Patti Edwards is purposeful about the opportunities students have to reassess after a whole-group assessment. At the start of the course, she shares with her students a visual aid that walks them through the entire assessment process, including paths for reassessment (see figure 4.1).

Notice how, before any reassessments take place, Patti expects students to first take notes and ask questions, complete practice problems, and develop a half sheet of formulas for students to show they are ready for reassessment. As part of this process, she also models the problems for her students. Once the class completes the assessment, she determines who needs to complete additional work to meet the assessed standards. For those students who will need to be reassessed, she engages in reteaching and instructs them to complete a journal. This journal is set up in two columns. In the first column, students rework incomplete or incorrect problems. In the second column, students explain why they missed the problems or explain their new thinking that improved their process. When a student has completed those two steps, Patti meets with him or her separately and schedules a time to complete the reassessment, which she conducts individually or in small groups, depending on what is most efficient. However, if she determines that a student has demonstrated

The Road to Success for Calculus

Take notes on examples; ask questions.

Work practice problems; ask questions.

Develop half a sheet of notes with formulas; ask questions.

Take the assessment on a learning target.

Work or rework more practice problems; ask questions; have a discussion with Mrs. Edwards.

Complete a journal on the learning target; discuss it with Mrs. Edwards.

Proceed to the next learning target.

Proceed to the next learning target.

Talk to Mrs. Edwards about your understanding and set up a reassessment time.

Take the reassessment on the learning target.

Proceed to the next learning target.

Source: © 2016 by Patti Edwards. Used with permission.

Figure 4.1: Example reassessment flowchart.

understanding and proficiency (metacognition) of the assessed standards through the journaling process, that student does not need to take the reassessment.

The reason for this approach is that students' frustration around reassessments can grow when teachers require them to jump through multiple steps that students perceive to be unnecessary toward learning the standard (Peters, Kruse, Buckmiller, & Townsley, 2017). In contrast, through journaling, students can more quickly and efficiently express their new learning to a teacher. Additionally, this approach allows for a quick conversation between the teacher and the student. Instead of students saying, "What do I need to do to get my grade up?" they would say, "Here is my new learning on this standard." In Patti's experience, students' responses to this method have been positive.

Students Should Have a Voice in How Relearning Takes Place

As figure 4.1 (page 75) makes clear, new learning must take place before reassessment. Giving students a voice in how that learning occurs can be an effective motivator for them to learn and demonstrate their new understanding (Garry, Fodchuk, & Hobbs, 2018). To give students a voice in their learning, teachers can require them to submit a relearning plan before reassessment, such as Patti Edwards's approach in figure 4.1. Educators and authors Fred Bramante and Rose Colby (2012) suggest, "only after the relearning plan is complete is the reassessment taken" (p. 72).

A relearning plan acts like an insurance policy or opportunity cost, so students are not just taking guesses through multiple reassessments. Similar to an insurance policy, this approach reassures students that they will receive another chance if their first attempt at learning crashes. The opportunity to do so comes at a cost, but not a punitive one. Instead, students may have to complete several tasks to simultaneously earn the opportunity to reassess and ensure they set themselves up for the strongest potential to succeed the next time. Students should not take any reassessment without demonstrating to the teacher that new learning has occurred. They should also have to provide evidence of the relearning. However, it's important that teachers give students flexibility in the mode they use to communicate that learning. This could include any or several of the following.

- Completing homework that was originally assigned but not previously completed

- Writing in a journal

- Conversing with the teacher

- Completing additional practice problems
- Engaging in a tutoring session
- Rereading lab procedures

These artifacts serve as a new check for evidence of understanding. Once the teacher feels the student has demonstrated a stronger level of learning based on this evidence, the student should have the opportunity to complete the formal reassessment.

Teachers with significant experience using standards-based grading note any plans that include multiple means and opportunities to demonstrate relearning must be *sustainable* over time. Students cannot be reassessing all the time, or else the teacher will quickly fall into a managerial nightmare. Solon High School biology teacher Dawn Posekany shares this reassessment process with her students:

> Students may reassess any learning target they want except those from the science fair project (first quarter) and fetal pig dissection test (second quarter), as long as they meet the deadlines for reassessment and complete the insurance policy. First, correct the part of the target test you want to reassess and go over the corrections with me. At this time, I may request or assign more practice. I will also check that you have a complete science notebook. You must complete any notes, homework, or any other missing work that may have caused the lower score.
>
> Once these requirements are met, you must schedule a time with me to reassess. Reassessment cannot be on the same day you received help from me, and you may reassess only one learning target per day. The reassessment is not identical to the original quiz or test. The new score replaces the previous score. Students may reassess as many times as necessary, but I may require you to complete additional practice or work with each attempt. (personal communication, September 12, 2013)

Note how Dawn clearly describes the evidence students must provide (correcting the test, completing all requested and assigned practice, and submitting notes) and then determines an appropriate reassessment time with the student. This relearning plan is well-communicated to students and permits them to have a voice in the process.

Teachers Should Have Multiple Ways of Assessing the Same Standard for Different Students

Just as students should have multiple ways to approach relearning, teachers need multiple ways to approach assessing the same learning standards. Educators and authors Carol Ann Tomlinson and Tanya R. Moon (2013) suggest teachers think about the usefulness of when an assessment should occur, what should be assessed, and when the assessment should take place. In thinking about multiple ways of assessing the same standard for different students, we find it is most important to consider *when* the assessment should take place. In this section, we highlight three strategies for this.

The first strategy is called *spiraling*, which is a form of distributed practice. Foreign language classes often refer to it as *the spacing effect* (Bahrick, Bahrick, Bahrick, & Bahrick, 1993). Solon High School Spanish teacher Karry Putzy uses spiraling as a way to give multiple assessments throughout the week. Most often, she gives brief quizzes on Monday, Wednesday, and Friday to assess the same learning standard. If a student is successful on one of the quizzes, they have shown mastery of the standard and don't need to repeat the assessment. If the student has not reached mastery on the standard through the quiz, then he or she will have opportunities later in the week to reassess. A student score later in the week replaces a previous score. Using this strategy, groups of students receive reteaching throughout the week of instruction.

A teacher might begin to spiral curriculum throughout the course to better utilize instructional time. For example, teachers can do this by using the last five to ten minutes at the end of each class period to reteach students who struggled on previous assessments. As another example, teachers can embed previous assessment items on future assessments. Not only does this practice allow the teacher to use this information as a built-in reassessment, but it also provides a way to spiral the curriculum to check for retention of important standards.

The second strategy teachers can use to assess the same standard for different students is product differentiation, which involves giving students an opportunity to show mastery in different ways. For example, let's say students are learning about the causes of the American Civil War in a U.S. history class. The teacher has three standards that every student must learn before the end of the unit. However, the teacher gives students a choice of two ways they can show understanding of these three course standards: (1) write a paper or (2) create a movie. Notice this approach works hand in hand with the need for students to have a voice in their relearning.

Earlier in this chapter, we examined how teacher Patti Edwards uses reassessments with her students (page 75). If you look back at that example, you will see that she also differentiates the products students must produce as evidence of their learning. Not every student who completes a reassessment in her room has to take another form of the test or quiz; some create a journal. This can also be a way for teachers to differentiate assessments. Some students may be able to demonstrate proficiency through reflective writing.

The third strategy for knowing when it is time to shake up instructional methods is maintaining a log of the number of times a student has completed optional reassessments. Not only does such a record help when communicating with parents about a student's progress (see the next criterion), but it also helps inform whether a teacher's instruction is making an impact on a student's learning.

Consider a student who has been taught multiple times how to do something but still doesn't get it. A reflective teacher will think about the ways he or she can modify future instruction to better help this student understand not just the current standard but future ones as well. By reflecting on what teaching and learning methods best work with a student, the teacher can also help identify if the student has a learning disability or other issue that an intervention team is better equipped to address. Let's say a teacher has modified assessment methods, and a student continues to score 1s and 2s on assessments using the five-level scale we introduced in chapter 2 (page 28). The teacher works closely with the student to reteach the material, and when it is time to have a formal reassessment, the student continues to score below mastery. As this pattern of not learning and falling further behind emerges, it is incumbent on the teacher to refer the student to the school's intervention team.

There are two ways teachers at Solon High School have found success in tracking the number of times a student reassesses. First, teachers list assessments in an old-fashioned checklist in a notebook or spreadsheet and keep track of how often students reassess. Second, teachers capture these data in a student information system. For example, in figure 4.2 (page 80), you can see the teacher has included notes in the comments section about how often the student reassessed a particular standard for students and parents to see. Emphasize for both students and parents that these data are a record of students' choosing to persevere with their learning and benefiting from that effort.

Teachers Should Communicate Information Related to Reteaching and Reassessment to Parents

It is essential that teachers communicate with parents and students regarding reassessment and reteaching opportunities that are available outside the classroom. Teachers need to keep parents in the know in the event they want to learn about opportunities their children will have to demonstrate learning beyond the initial assessment date and, in turn, improve their grades. Similarly, self-motivated students

Course	English Language Arts 10
Standard	Short-Story Quizzes: Making Inferences
Due Date	1/23
Comments	1/20: "MDG" quiz—3 (initial assessment) / 3 (reassessment) 1/22: "Roman Fever" quiz—2 (initial assessment) / 3 (reassessment) 1/23: "The Interlopers" quiz—3 (initial assessment) / 3 (reassessment) 2/18: "Thanks, Ma'am" quiz—1 (initial assessment) / 3 (reassessment) 2/19: "The Sniper" quiz—3 (initial assessment) / 3 (reassessment) Changed the score to a 3 after assessments on 2/18–2/19

Source: © 2015 by Jim Erickson. Used with permission.

Figure 4.2: Electronic gradebook comments section documenting reassessment attempts.

who wish to seek out additional learning opportunities to improve their assessed grade following the initial assessment will want to know the reassessment procedures available to them.

There are two non-negotiables regarding this communication. First, teachers must include information about reassessment and reteaching procedures in an email to parents or in the course syllabus at the beginning of each reporting period. However, including this information in just an email or a syllabus is not always enough, because not everyone will read it! Teachers using standards-based grading should strive to overcommunicate. Figure 4.3 shows a sample letter that Lauren Cannon, a Solon High School social studies teacher, has used to communicate her practices. Office staff help mail these letters to ensure that parents receive a copy.

The second non-negotiable is that teachers must inform parents and students of the final relearning deadline. Even with standards-based grading, there is an endpoint, and it is important to establish a cutoff date for final reassessments so that teachers may submit their grades on time at the end of each reporting period. For example, if teachers must submit their end-of-semester grades by January 10 at 4:00 p.m., it is unrealistic for students to be completing reassessments up until 3:59 p.m. on that date because it does not allow enough time for grading. A more reasonable approach is for teachers to determine a final reassessment cutoff date several days before the end of reporting to permit enough time for grading and data entry. Teacher teams at Solon High School have settled on one of the following deadlines for all reassessments. Both have benefits, and deciding on an end date may depend on the content area.

Solon Community School District

Dear Parents,

I am so excited to be working with your student this quarter. The purpose of this letter is to provide some insight into what your student will be learning about in advanced psychology, my classroom expectations, and my grading procedures.

Course Description

The study of psychology allows students to gain understandings into the complexities of human thought and behavior and the factors related to the differences between people. This course, geared toward juniors and seniors, is designed for students interested in further study in the field of psychology. This course will move quickly through child development, social psychology, abnormal psychology, and sensation and perception. The goals of this class include stimulating your interest in and expanding your knowledge of the field of psychology. Emphasis will be placed on evaluation, analysis, and application of course topics to everyday life.

Standards or Learning Targets

The majority of the entries you will find in PowerSchool will be aligned with daily learning targets you can find on my classroom website (https://sites .google.com/a/solon.k12.ia.us/cannon-s-class-2013-2014/home). One learning target that will appear on an upcoming assessment is "I can use Piaget's theory of cognitive development to describe how children think at specific stages." It is listed in PowerSchool as "Cognitive Development." Every day, we focus on one of these targets, and your child is given an opportunity to practice meeting the learning targets during in-class assignments. Eventually, your child will have the opportunity to demonstrate his or her learning in a classroom assessment. These assessments begin with comprehension questions that are based on facts and concepts that we learned and end with questions that require higher-order-thinking skills.

Grade Scale

Below, you will find the grade scale that I use to gauge student achievement on learning targets. In order to score a 4, students will need to make novel connections, employ higher-order-thinking skills, and demonstrate a complete and thorough understanding of the learning target. This does not mean their answer is perfect. Rather, it shows that they not only know the learning target but also can reason, evaluate, and make connections with ideas that they hear about on the news or that they have learned in other classes.

Source: © 2014 by Lauren Cannon and Solon High School. Used with permission.

Figure 4.3: Sample letter to parents.

- Most departments set a deadline to have all reassessments completed one week before the end of the term. The reason for this deadline is twofold. First, it allows the teacher a manageable amount of time to assess student work before the end of the term. Second, the students still receive feedback on standards before the final exam.

- The language arts department sets a deadline to have all reassessments completed two weeks prior to the end of the term. This is partly because several of these reassessments can be student papers. Again, a manageable deadline for completing assessments is important for both the teacher and students.

In some instances, teachers will need to extend the deadline beyond the grading term for some students to be able to complete reassessments. This happens on a case-by-case basis when students have an educational need that carries past the end of the term. In these cases, Solon High School gives the student an incomplete grade, and that student works with the teacher to establish a plan to reassess course material. These requests only come from the teacher and can include students who missed significant amounts of instruction during the grading term due to sickness or other factors.

Regardless of the deadline, it is important to communicate the reassessment deadline to both parents and students. Ideally, teachers should include this information in their communication at the start of the reporting period as well as in the syllabus.

Reassessment Opportunities Should Be Both Teacher- and Student-Initiated

Before we look at the differences between teacher-initiated and student-initiated reassessments, it is important to understand the need to establish a schoolwide schedule that allows for reassessments. Early in our implementation at Solon High School, we communicated to students in each class the schedule for reassessments. As part of its daily schedule, the school has thirty minutes of seminar (homeroom) time Monday through Friday. Before our standards-based grading implementation, we mostly used this as a study hall. However, once we implemented standards-based grading, we began to use this time for reassessments. So, teachers gave students a choice to reassess either before school, after school, or during seminar. Occasionally, teachers would meet with students during their prep period, but ideally, teachers should reserve this time for planning instruction, aligning standards, and creating assessments.

Figure 4.4 provides a look at a typical day at Solon High School. The school is on a four-by-four block schedule. In this system, rather than students enrolling in eight forty-two-minute class periods per day, students attend just four eighty-four-minute classes per day. The middle of the day includes a thirty-minute lunch and a thirty-minute seminar. Because the school year is broken up into four forty-five-day quarters, students complete yearlong courses, such as algebra 1 or biology, in a semester.

Regular Day		
	Start Time	**End Time**
First Block	8:20 a.m.	9:44 a.m.
Second Block	9:49 a.m.	11:13 a.m.
Lunch or Seminar	11:16 a.m.	11:46 a.m.
Lunch or Seminar	11:48 a.m.	12:18 p.m.
Third Block	12:22 p.m.	1:46 p.m.
Fourth Block	1:51 p.m.	3:15 p.m.

Figure 4.4: Example class schedule.

Along with including the teachers' reassessment schedules in their syllabi, we supported our collaborative PLC philosophy by creating a schoolwide matrix showing the times that all teachers are available. It's common for students that need reteaching and reassessment in one content area to also need simultaneous support in one or more different content areas. By establishing this matrix, we helped ensure transparency across our building so students would not have to choose between subjects. It allowed us to spread out our resources.

During collaboration time, teachers proactively plan the future in order to provide specific times during and outside the school day when students can receive additional time and support. For example, in mathematics, where students often needed extra time for reassessments, we purposefully staggered our schedule so that a mathematics teacher had time at the end of each block to help students for five or ten minutes. We also staggered teacher lunch and homeroom time so that a teacher in the content area was available during all times of the school day. This coplanning among teachers allows them to arrange varied periods of availability in their schedules so students can receive help from a teacher in the relevant department while limiting scheduling conflicts. Figure 4.5 (page 84) shows our buildingwide teacher availability for reassessments. At Solon High School, we included a link to this matrix on our school's webpage so that parents have easy access to this information.

Teacher	Before-School Time	Seminar A	Seminar B	After-School Time	Open Time	Final Reassessment Deadline
Goerend	Available 7:50–8:20 a.m.	Not available	Available	Available 3:15–4:05 p.m.	First block	The last week of the quarter
Dearborn	Available by appointment	Available	Available by appointment	Available until 4:30 p.m.	First block	The last week of the quarter
Beattie	Available 7:50–8:20 a.m.	Available	Not available	Only after October 14 due to coaching	Fourth block	Two weeks after the initial assessment
Woodring	Available 7:40–8:15 a.m.	Available	Available	Not available	Available by appointment during third block	Two weeks after the initial assessment
McSweeney	Available by appointment	Not available	Available	Available by appointment	Contact school office to identify open teaching times.	The last week of the quarter
Hemsath	Available 7:30–8:15 a.m.	Available	Available	Available 3:15–4:00 p.m.	Fourth block	Three weeks after the initial assessment is returned to the student
Grandgenett	Available 8:00–8:15 a.m.	Available	Available	Available 3:15–4:00 p.m. by appointment only	Third block	Two weeks after the initial assessment is returned to the student
Johnson	Available 7:45–8:15 a.m.	Available	Available	Contact teacher first to set up appointment.	Third block	One week before the last day of the quarter

Figure 4.5: Example schoolwide matrix of teachers' availability for reassessments.

Having a highly accessible tool for scheduling reassessment time enables both teachers and students to initiate and schedule reassessments. It's important to understand that no matter who initiates the reassessment process, the reassessments themselves remain the same; for example, a teacher or a student could initiate completion of a mathematics journal. What differs is the process for initiating the reassessment. Also note that the final reassessment deadlines in figure 4.5 are set by the department and not individual teachers. Within course types, the final reassessment policy is consistent for all students.

A teacher-initiated reassessment is one that the teacher *requires* students (all students, a select individual, or a select group) to complete. Because teachers in a PLC strive to direct students to additional learning opportunities (DuFour, 2004), teacher-initiated reassessments should be the norm, and student participation is not optional. Often, this reassessment follows a formative assessment where the teacher determined a large portion of students didn't understand the learning target. This type of reassessment is often done as a whole class during regular class time.

A student-initiated reassessment is one in which a student requests a reassessment opportunity from the teacher. Teachers should accept student-initiated requests pending the student has met any required relearning plan criteria. However, to reassess, students have to meet the insurance-policy requirements or fulfill the opportunity cost the teacher has established (see page 76). For example, let's look at a middle school social studies class. After the class has completed an assessment on a standard related to the causes and effects of World War I, a student finds he or she scored at level 2 of understanding (on a 0–4 scale) of the standard. The teacher determines that most of the class has a proficient understanding of that standard and will be moving on to the next standard. There will be no in-class reteaching of that concept. At this point, the student can initiate a reassessment with the teacher by completing the steps the teacher identified in the class relearning plan.

Having a clear reassessment policy allows teachers to determine when they can move to the next standard while an individual student or a group of students go back to demonstrate further understanding. Figure 4.6 (page 86) provides a visual of the steps teachers should follow when engaging in standards-based assessment and teacher- and student-initiated reassessment.

Note that we detail the role of a teacher team in developing reassessment policies in this chapter's PLC Connection section (page 88).

The teacher goes back to the first step if he or she determines most students require additional instruction and activities.

Students participate in classroom instruction and activities based on course or grade-level standards.

The teacher facilitates classroom feedback and conducts an informal assessment.

The process starts over, and the teacher begins teaching new course or grade-level standards.

All students participate in one or more formal assessments.

Students receive feedback on assessment results.
The teacher puts the scores into the gradebook.

Some students may still not have demonstrated an understanding of course or grade-level standards.

The student or students initiate reassessment.

The teacher initiates reassessment.

The student or students meet requirements established by the teacher (such as completing initial homework or practice, attending an individual or group tutoring session, journaling, doing additional reading, or completing practice problems) to better understand course or grade-level standards.

The teacher provides additional instruction and activities to help the student or students better understand course or grade-level standards.

The individual student or small group of students participate in a reassessment opportunity.

This process repeats if necessary.

Figure 4.6: Standards-based grading assessment and reassessment flowchart.

Teachers Should Build in Classroom Time for Reteaching Before Students Reassess

Teachers should be careful not to rely on students' completing reassessments solely outside of class hours. A mix of direct instruction, guided practice, followed by independent practice during a lesson, will allow teachers to reteach to individuals or small groups as needed during the practice time at the end of the class period. In addition to providing time outside of class, teachers should find time during instruction to formatively assess, reteach, and provide reassessments. If teachers only provide time for students outside of class, scheduling reassessments will quickly become a problem.

We've heard from many teachers that class time is at a premium and that they don't have any room for the reteaching and reassessment we propose here. We assure you, these are both possible and essential. Joel Foreman teaches music at Solon High School and does an excellent job using class time to reteach in small groups and differentiate instruction. His vocal program has more than 160 students in three performing choirs and four small vocal jazz ensembles. During class, Joel uses a combination of three- to five-minute assessments to determine students' level of proficiency. He uses vocal warm-ups to quickly assess his students, similar to how a mathematics teacher uses a word problem of the day. Through these quick assessments, Joel can select from a variety of class standards, such as sight-singing, pitch, tone, or musical memorization, as his baseline for assessment and provide immediate feedback to students.

During instruction, Joel often stops to provide feedback based on his assessments. For example, while the concert choir sings a piece, he may stop and have the sopranos sing by themselves to assess their pitch. He will then work with this small group to provide reteaching and feedback. Later in the lesson, he will have the tenors sing the next verse of lines to check if the group can stay on pitch.

Even though this is a music class, teachers in other disciplines can replicate this same type of process. To compare this process to a core academic discipline, consider an example for a physics class lesson on force. Instead of testing for pitch, as in the music class, the teacher might ask students to draw a visual on their individual whiteboards, depicting their understanding of the concept. This quick assessment gives the science teacher a firm understanding of where each student is at before advancing in the lesson or moving on to a new standard.

Teachers experienced in using standards-based grading have found that by doing smaller and more frequent assessments, they can provide targeted reteaching and instruction when needed. They also find that their planning, instruction, and assessment become more purposeful, which results in more focused planning for small group reteaching (Knight & Cooper, 2019).

PLC Connection

Although individual teachers can accomplish a number of the aforementioned criteria, teams of teachers functioning within a schoolwide or districtwide PLC are best equipped to provide students with multiple opportunities to demonstrate their understanding. Here's why: teams can prevent the inconsistency that frequently occurs when teachers approach reassessment implementation individually (Peters et al., 2017; Webber Alder, 2019). With the best intentions in mind, individual teachers create their reassessment policies and communicate them to students and parents, yet students and parents may perceive the policies as being too different from one another, creating uncertainty about a school's approach to reassessment. For example, one teacher may require students to finish incomplete homework prior to reassessment while another teacher does not, or a teacher at one end of the building may require students to complete reassessments during class only while another provides flexibility during the day based on student and teacher availability.

The purpose of this section is to provide teacher teams with practical steps for collaboratively creating reassessment policies as well as suggest a realistic timeline for reassessments to occur. For example, English collaborative teacher teams may have reassessment timelines that last for nearly the entire length of the course. A student may be able to revise and reassess a paper from week one. However, a mathematics collaborative teacher team may want to set a two-week reassessment timeline so that students don't fall behind in the sequence of the course.

When a team meets to consider the third critical question of a PLC—How will we respond when some students do not learn?—the conversation often turns toward identifying gaps in student understanding according to the standards, which may occur following the whole-class summative assessment. To tackle this question, a team must develop a unified reassessment policy. This maximizes the potential for consistency across the team and ensures fewer students fall through the cracks. Teams should consider their responses to four important questions when writing their reassessment policies.

1. Which students need reassessment?

2. What criteria must students meet to demonstrate readiness for a reassessment?

3. When will students receive reassessment opportunities?

4. What parameters are in place to promote student and teacher time management?

By looking at the gradebook, teachers can identify students in need of reassessment. For example, a team of teachers at Solon Middle School identified any student who had a 2 or below (on a five-level scale) and concluded any student in that range should be required to participate in the reteaching and reassessment process.

All teachers should collaboratively establish criteria that students must meet prior to completing a reassessment. As part of these criteria, experienced standards-based grading teachers look at student homework completion aligned with the standards to be reassessed. If students have not completed the corresponding homework assignment (or assignments), the students must first complete it. Next, teachers typically assign students to a reteaching opportunity, coupled with even more opportunities to practice. For example, a middle school science student might be required to watch a review video about the scientific method and then respond to a teacher-provided writing prompt. Once the student meets these criteria, he or she becomes eligible to complete a reassessment.

Teachers creating a reassessment policy must also determine when students will receive reassessment opportunities. Depending on the school schedule and community norms for when students can come in (how early or how late), teams of teachers may need to think inside and outside the box. For example, some schools have created an intervention time during the school day. Others utilize class time or before- or after-school hours in addition to an intervention period. Because the times may change each week in some cases, Tim Sheeley, science teacher and coach at Solon Middle School, updates his whiteboard every week, communicating his availability before and after school to assist students.

Teacher teams should consider coordinating their availability to their own students as well as when they may be able to support students who are not on their class roster (for the purpose of lending support to other teachers). Frequently, creating an intervention time at the secondary level, if one does not already exist, may require revising the master schedule. Although this may be outside an individual team's purview, Buffum et al. (2012) note that shortening each class period by only a few minutes can easily create a thirty-minute tutorial period, which can simultaneously be used for enrichment activities too. All students can benefit from this intervention time.

Teams of teachers should consider a time frame for the reassessment process when writing their reassessment policies. Although it would be ideal to give students unlimited days to complete reassessments, calendars and the reality of an eight- to nine-hour workday suggest a finite number of opportunities exist for students to complete the reassessment process.

A middle school teacher we worked with proposed the idea of using student planners to keep track of and record reassessment requests for students. During homeroom each week, teachers would mark in student planners the students requested for teacher-initiated intervention and reassessment. Through the collaborative nature of a PLC, teachers across all teams used the planners to facilitate the creation of a schoolwide reassessment schedule that allowed for certain grade levels and content areas to meet for reassessments. Students would have check-ins with a content teacher, and the teachers would prioritize reassessment by standards and give students additional instruction. Using a system like this scaffolds the reassessment process so that students do not need to wait until near the end of the reporting period to attempt reassessment on multiple standards. Teachers appreciated this system because they believed it helped students better stay on track.

When writing a team reassessment policy, teacher teams also need to consider how many standards students can reassess each day or week as well as the time available inside and outside of class to provide the necessary supports for students. For example, a team of reading teachers at the middle school agreed students could only reassess one standard per week; this gave them ample time to reteach as well as time to provide feedback on the reassessments (in the event further reteaching and reassessment were needed). From the student perspective, this helped them prioritize their time and focus on reassessing a single standard rather than being overwhelmed by the total number of standards they were attempting.

After teams have discussed the four reassessment policy questions, they should next write a team-developed reassessment policy. A sample reassessment policy is as follows.

In order to reassess, students must complete any incomplete homework assignments related to the standard. In addition, the students must attend a tutorial session during the last ten minutes of class or during eighth-period intervention time. Once these requirements are met, the students may reassess. Reassessments are only available during eighth period on Mondays, Wednesdays, and Fridays in Mr. Smith's classroom. Only one standard may be assessed per week. The new score (1–4) replaces the old one. Students may reassess as many times as necessary; however, additional practice or tutorial work may be required with each attempt.

Building a consistent team, department, or grade-level communication plan can be challenging; however, once a team develops its assessment policy, the team should not merely communicate this plan to students. The team also needs to communicate the reassessment policy to parents. If anything, teachers should overcommunicate this information through course syllabi, parent letters, teacher websites, parent-teacher conferences, newsletters, and any other method the school utilizes to communicate with parents.

After teams develop and communicate their reassessment policy, a final step for them is to formalize a struggling learner identification protocol that they can regularly discuss and analyze at team meetings. The purpose of such a protocol is to identify struggling learners, communicate with them regarding the standards they need additional support in, change instruction for them, and communicate all of this information to parents. The collaborative culture of a PLC, with its emphasis on knowing what students have learned and the need to have plans to support those who haven't, makes it particularly well-suited for developing an identification protocol. Figure 4.7 (pages 92–93) shows an example of how a team of high school mathematics teachers collaborated to address struggling learners after an assessment.

Following the completion of a team-developed reassessment policy, teachers in a PLC will have a consistent approach to providing multiple opportunities for struggling students to demonstrate understanding. Note that this collaborative work must be an ongoing process. During team collaboration time, teachers should frequently discuss the effectiveness of the existing reassessment policy and consider ideas to improve its effectiveness. For example, if a large number of students is assigned to a tutorial session for a particular standard, the team may decide to address any misconceptions during class to free up time for more individualized tutorial and reassessment needs. Because teams in a PLC strive to utilize collective commitments and a shared purpose (DuFour et al., 2008; DuFour et al., 2016), teachers will hold each other accountable to implementing a reassessment policy that meets the needs of the school's unique learners.

Common Pitfalls When Providing Students Multiple Opportunities to Demonstrate Their Learning

Along with the six criteria teams need to meet to give students multiple opportunities to demonstrate their understanding, secondary educators should be aware of several pitfalls to avoid. These pitfalls include the following.

- Allowing students to reassess without demonstrating new understanding

Teacher and Class	Number and Percentage of Students Who Are Not Yet Proficient	Number and Percentage of Students Who Are Almost Proficient	Number and Percentage of Students Who Have Demonstrated Understanding
Hayes, period 2, algebra 1	9 students, 39 percent	8 students, 35 percent	6 students, 26 percent
Hayes, period 3, algebra 1	8 students, 32 percent	13 students, 52 percent	4 students, 16 percent
Muhayimana, period 5, algebra 2	11 students, 46 percent	9 students, 38 percent	4 students, 17 percent
Gilson, period 1, algebra 2	10 students, 59 percent	5 students, 29 percent	2 students, 12 percent
Gilson, period 3, algebra 2	13 students, 62 percent	6 students, 29 percent	2 students, 10 percent
Schares, period 6, statistics	6 students, 85 percent	1 student, 15 percent	0 students, 0 percent
Huckstadt, period 1, geometry	22 students, 100 percent	0 students, 0 percent	0 students, 0 percent
Huckstadt, period 3, precalculus	4 students, 33 percent	4 students, 33 percent	4 students, 33 percent

Consider how we will respond to students who experienced difficulty and how we will respond to students who have already demonstrated understanding. To help determine these responses, answer the following guiding questions.

- Did one class have significantly better results than the others? If so, did that class use any different instructional strategies?

No. For the most part, students at higher levels of mathematics did better, but no one class did significantly better than the others.

- Were many students below proficiency? If so, consider revisiting core instruction.

Yes. However, we believe we understand the reasons for this. (See the next response.)

- What is the team's hypothesis for why students did not meet proficiency?

  Algebra had not yet covered the assessed concept, geometry had just finished the instruction the day prior, and some of the higher-level students did not put forth 100 percent effort.

- What is the team's hypothesis for why students met or exceeded proficiency?

  Students who met or exceeded proficiency had recent exposure to the concepts and are high-ability students who pick up concepts easily.

- What instructional strategies do team members suggest using to reteach this standard?

  Incorporate graphing and the algebra approach. Consider hands-on activities to apply the concepts.

	Students Identified for Intervention, Practice, or Enrichment	Planned Instructional Strategy
Additional Time and Support	*All students below proficiency*	*Small-group reteaching, Geometer's Sketchpad, IXL online resources, ALEKS online tutoring and assessment*
Additional Practice	*Students at proficiency*	*Geometer's Sketchpad, IXL online resources, ALEKS online tutoring and assessment, worksheet or activity, peer teaching*
Enrichment	*Highly proficient students*	*Applied problems or activity*

Figure 4.7: Sample team protocol for identifying and addressing struggling learners.

*Visit **go.SolutionTree.com/PLCbooks** for a free reproducible version of this figure.*

- Establishing an open-door reassessment policy that is not manageable over a long period
- Inconsistently communicating reassessment opportunities and practices to parents and students
- Requiring students to complete all reassessments outside of class
- Averaging reassessment scores when entering them in the gradebook

The following sections describe these pitfalls and how you can avoid them.

Allowing Students to Reassess Without Demonstrating New Understanding

In the early stages of implementation, we often see teachers make the common mistake of not requiring students to demonstrate new understanding *before* allowing them to reassess. Nathan remembers the first day he talked to students about standards-based grading. As principal, he stood in front of each class of students and explained how homework was not going to count as part of their grade. He shared research, cited articles, and highlighted best practices. Consequently, the message students received was, "The principal said we don't have to do any homework! *Yes!* This is the best school ever!" As you can imagine, the knock-on effects from this were numerous.

Following these first meetings, students attempted *no* practice activities and struggled on the initial assessment. From their perspective, if they did poorly, then they could just hope to guess better on the next assessment or the one after that. There was no need to engage in their learning through homework or practice assignments. After a couple of weeks of struggling through this problem, teachers in the school presented additional information about the requirements students had to meet to *earn* the opportunity to reassess. In this case, those additional requirements came in the form of the insurance policies and opportunity costs we discussed earlier in this chapter (page 76). This meant that students had to do something to be eligible to reassess. They needed to have some skin in the game, which is something they came to appreciate. Findings in other standards-based grading implementations also align with this experience (Peters et al., 2017).

Establishing an Open-Door Reassessment Policy That Is Not Manageable Over a Long Period

As early adopters of standards-based grading have likely experienced, having an open-door policy for students creates a lot of headaches for teachers. Permitting students to initiate reassessments anytime and on any day, prior to reteaching, does not set up students for success as they have not done the work to increase their level of understanding of standards before engaging with the follow-up attempts. This creates extra grading on the teachers' part and additional follow-up work for the student as well. Instead, a better-planned approach to reassessment is needed to create efficiency over time.

Matt recalls a conversation he had with a third-year teacher early in his implementation of standards-based grading. The teacher had been an early adopter and felt that the shift toward standards-based grading practices would better help his students understand the learning targets for his class. In the conversation, he talked about his frustrations with reassessment deadlines and his desire to have an open-door policy so students could reassess whenever they wanted. Rather than highlight the pitfalls inherent in this approach, the author encouraged the teacher to try that method and follow up with him after a few assessments. When the teacher checked back in with the author a couple of weeks later, he said his opinion on an open-door policy had quickly changed. In thinking he was supporting students' needs, he had soon found himself in an organizational nightmare he couldn't keep up with. Handfuls of student reassessments were piling up on the teacher's desk, many of them unsuccessful attempts at learning. At the same time, these students were falling behind in their understanding of concepts in class that were building on prerequisite knowledge. Without a system in place, student frustrations were growing right along with the stack of papers for the teacher to grade. This is not a positive combination.

The important point to take away from this example is that teachers need a detailed process for reassessments. Rather than having an open-door policy for students to reassess when they choose, teachers must set clear expectations for *what* students need to do, *when* they need to do it, and *how* they can initiate a reassessment. Furthermore, a reassessment policy should be a collaborative effort across teams so that practices are consistent from classroom to classroom. (Refer to the PLC Connection for this chapter, page 88.)

Inconsistently Communicating Reassessment Opportunities and Practices to Parents and Students

Initially, it might appear sensible to have every classroom teacher communicate the importance of the reassessment process. Although this may seem like a good idea, it will cause problems if teachers do not all communicate a common message or vocabulary. At Solon High School, when we first began the implementation of reassessment opportunities, every teacher communicated the message differently. Instead of trying to standardize our school practices, we created an organizational nightmare for students and parents. Students were unable to keep track of each teacher's individual reassessment process and deadlines, and a small group of parents began to express their frustration due to this lack of information. Having the foundation to ensure consistent practices for grading are clearly communicated to students and parents is critical to making sure the reassessment process is coordinated across all grade levels and content areas.

There are many ways to accomplish this. Some school districts use their electronic mass-communication system to deliver important videos and letters that document schoolwide reassessment procedures. We suggest that whatever form of communication you use, it expresses a clear understanding of what reassessment does and does not mean. For example, you might suggest that reassessment means the following.

- Students learn different subjects at varying rates; therefore, students who did not demonstrate understanding by _____ should be allowed to demonstrate understanding at a later date.

- Teachers will provide individual students with additional opportunities to demonstrate understanding after the final regularly scheduled whole-group assessment for that specific standard. This can take place during class, study hall, seminar, or outside of regular school hours. See the schoolwide schedule listed on our website.

- Teachers will consider utilizing multiple ways of assessing the same standard for different students.

- Teachers will provide required new learning opportunities before students complete a reassessment.

Conversely, the following might constitute a list of what reassessment *does not* mean.

- Students will not be permitted to reassess without first completing additional learning opportunities individually or with the teacher, a peer, or a parent.

- Teachers will not have the option not to reassess a student who has met the requirements of the class' relearning plan. In our school, reassessments are required to be offered under the teacher's relearning plan.

- Grading periods will not change or be eliminated, nor will grades be changed after the end of a grading period.

- Students will not have to reassess if they have already demonstrated a high level of understanding of a standard on a previous assessment. Teachers will provide reassessments only in the specific areas for which a student has not yet demonstrated understanding.

Requiring Students to Complete All Reassessments Outside of Class

Requiring students to complete all reassessments outside of class may sound good in theory, but we found it lost its luster in practice. We learned about this pitfall when we realized that there simply wasn't enough time to manage the number of reassessments and the amount of work that standards-based grading created. To address this problem, we developed a two-fold solution that prevented us from requiring students to complete reassessments outside of class: (1) as we previously discussed, our teachers better utilized class time for reteaching, and (2) our work as a PLC helped us create a systemwide intervention period during the school day. These steps ensured we had a schoolwide process to identify students targeted for reassessments and that we had built additional teaching opportunities into our school day.

We also found that, when additional flexibility was offered in some categorical state funding, the high school staff strongly supported hiring a success coordinator position. This newly created position played an important role in co-coordinating the schoolwide intervention period with the principal. As a result, nearly 75 percent of students that high school teachers requested for intervention were placed in an appropriate intervention during the school day. Schools without the ability to add a position such as this may choose to modify this solution to meet their unique needs. For example, a school may choose to add an intervention period once every other week on Fridays to begin supporting students who have not yet demonstrated understanding.

Regardless of the resources available, schools should consider changes to their master schedule to ensure students have time during the school day to engage in class relearning plans. See the Developing a Master Schedule section in chapter 5 (page 118) for additional support.

Averaging Reassessment Scores When Entering Them in the Gradebook

Be wary of averaging reassessment scores. Because we know students learn in different ways and on different days, averaging multiple assessment attempts at the same standard puts later learners at a disadvantage. As we've established, the purpose of grades is to communicate students' *current* levels of learning; therefore, students who learn at different rates should receive similar marks in the gradebook. As a certified educator, you are trained in assessment, so instead of averaging a student's scores, use your best judgment when making a determination. It may be tempting to rely on descriptive statistics and other algorithms provided by electronic gradebooks; however, these methods are no more accurate or reliable in communicating learning when compared to trusting teachers' judgment (Guskey & Jung, 2016).

Let's examine a case where averaging gives you the wrong information about what a student has learned. For the sake of this example, we will use a five-level scale, with 0–1 communicating little to no evidence of learning, 2 being an area of concern, and 3–4 indicating proficiency. Assume the following sample student scores are for a single standard in your class for which the student has reassessed four times.

Standard 1: 1, 1, 2, and 4

Picture these scores as entered into the gradebook chronologically from left to right. If you do the descriptive statistics, you would have an average of 2, a median of 1.5, and a mode of 1. Instead of averaging, think about these questions: Has the student mastered the standard? What is his or her level of proficiency on the *most recent* assessments? When you examine these scores, you see that the student began making measurable progress on the third reassessment and achieved mastery of the learning standards with the fourth assessment. In a standards-based classroom, this student should earn a score of 4 on the scale.

Assessment Tools for Your Journey

The major purpose of this chapter is to describe how to provide students with multiple opportunities to demonstrate their understanding, which is the third standards-based grading principle. Figure 4.8 and figure 4.9 (page 101) show the standards-based grading continuum for this principle. Figure 4.8 is for individual teachers to fill out. Once each teacher has assessed him- or herself, the team should use figure 4.9 to assess itself. (See pages 140 and 144 for reproducible versions of these continua.) Departments, leadership teams, and entire schools may use the self-reported levels of implementation for each standards-based grading guideline to plan their next implementation supports.

Directions: As an individual, circle each criterion that aligns with your current level of implementation of the third standards-based grading principle—students should have multiple opportunities to demonstrate their learning. Consider the evidence following the criteria as examples of artifacts you or other team members can provide or share with each other as well as other teams in your PLC. Note it is possible to circle criteria from multiple categories.

Getting Started	Implementing	Sustaining
Criteria: I sometimes, but not always, provide students with an opportunity to complete assessment opportunities after the final regularly scheduled whole-group assessment.	**Criteria:** I provide individual students with additional opportunities to demonstrate understanding after the final regularly scheduled whole-group assessment. The additional opportunities may be based on the entire assessment or on specific standards.	**Criteria:** I provide individual students with additional opportunities to demonstrate understanding after the final regularly scheduled whole-group assessment. The additional opportunities are based on specific standards.

Figure 4.8: Continuum for standards-based grading principle 3—individual assessment.

continued ▶

Getting Started	Implementing	Sustaining
I do not yet have a plan in place that allows all students multiple opportunities to demonstrate their understanding of classroom standards in various ways. Teacher-initiated spiraling is currently the only form of reassessment I use in my classroom. I do not reteach in small groups, differentiate instruction, or provide an alternate way of learning before a student reassesses.	I have a plan in place that allows all students multiple opportunities to demonstrate their understanding of classroom standards in various ways; however, I am not sure if it is sustainable over time. Reassessment opportunities are either only teacher initiated or only student initiated. I sometimes reteach in small groups, differentiate instruction, or provide an alternate way of learning before a student reassesses. I have communicated information related to reteaching and reassessment to parents, such as via a course syllabus.	I have a plan in place that allows all students multiple opportunities to demonstrate their understanding of classroom standards in various ways, and I regularly review this plan to ensure it is sustainable over time. Reassessment opportunities are both teacher and student initiated. For example, students are allowed to initiate reassessment opportunities on any assessment that was looped (teacher initiated) during the term. I have built time into my class instruction to reteach in small groups, differentiate instruction, and provide an alternate way of learning before a student reassesses. I have communicated information related to reteaching and reassessment to parents in multiple ways, such as via a course syllabus and course website.

Evidence: Reassessment opportunities are not yet present. I have not yet documented a teacher reassessment plan. Reteaching or small-group instruction is not evident in lesson plans.	**Evidence:** Some, but not all, student assessments are targeted to specific standards. I lack comfort with my teacher reassessment plan, and it includes only either teacher- or student-initiated opportunities. Reteaching or small-group instruction is evident in lesson plans.	**Evidence:** Student reassessments are targeted to specific standards. I am very comfortable with my teacher reassessment plan, which includes teacher- and student-initiated opportunities. Students complete a learning (insurance) plan before reassessment opportunities. Reteaching or small-group instruction is evident in lesson plans and observable during daily instruction.

Directions: As a team, circle each criterion that aligns with your team's current level of implementation of the third standards-based grading principle—students should have multiple opportunities to demonstrate their learning. Consider the evidence following the criteria as examples of artifacts your team members can provide or share with each other as well as other teams in your PLC. Note it is possible to circle criteria from multiple categories.

Getting Started	Implementing	Sustaining
Criteria: Teachers on our team have not created reassessment policies.	**Criteria:** Some, but not all, of the teachers on our team have created a reassessment policy.	**Criteria:** Our team has a unified reassessment policy based on the three important questions.
Evidence: No reassessment policies exist.	**Evidence:** Reassessment policies exist, but individual reassessment policies on the team differ significantly from one another.	**Evidence:** The single team-developed reassessment policy communicates the criteria students must meet to demonstrate readiness for a reassessment, when the students receive reassessment opportunities, and the parameters necessary to promote student and teacher time management.

Figure 4.9: Continuum for standards-based grading principle 3—team assessment.

After completing both the individual and team assessments, use the action-plan template in figure 4.10 to write down your and your team's current levels of implementation and next steps. (See page 151 for a reproducible version of this action-plan template.)

My current level on the continuum for the third standards-based grading principle—students should have multiple opportunities to demonstrate their learning—is best described as (circle one):

Getting started   **Implementing**   **Sustaining**

Evidence I can provide to support my current level includes:

My next steps will be:

My team's current level on the continuum for the third standards-based grading principle—students should have multiple opportunities to demonstrate their learning—is best described as (circle one):

Getting started   **Implementing**   **Sustaining**

Evidence my team can provide to support our current level includes:

Directions: Use the following table to plan your team's next steps.

Desired Level and Criteria: Where do we want to be?	**Action:** What do we need to do to move closer to sustaining on the standards-based grading continuum for this principle?	**Change:** What do we need to change or give up?	**Evidence of Success:** What products, policies, or procedures would demonstrate our desired criteria?

Figure 4.10: Action-plan template for standards-based grading principle 3.

CHAPTER 5

Criteria for Administrators and Leaders Implementing Standards-Based Grading

Once administrators and other leaders make the decision to use standards-based grading practices across the school or district, they need to establish and communicate a multiyear implementation plan. This cannot be an overnight (or over-summer) implementation. Experience from a number of schools suggests rushed, inconsistent, and poorly communicated standards-based grading implementation is a root cause of parent and community pushback (Peters & Buckmiller, 2014; Webber Alder, 2019).

Although school leaders may think it appealing to attend a motivational workshop or conduct a three-month book study and then announce, "Next year, we are implementing standards-based grading," the complexities of the change suggest this approach may cause discomfort for a variety of stakeholders. Standards-based grading involves what Tim Waters, Robert J. Marzano, and Brian McNulty (2003) describe as *second-order change* because it implies a significant break with past practices that requires looking at established structures in new manners. It asks that educators, students, and parents see gradebooks and report cards in a completely different way. Therefore, standards-based grading implementation takes careful planning, exceptional communication, and well-planned professional learning for teachers and school leaders to anticipate and overcome common roadblocks.

Specifically, this chapter details the five key criteria schools and districts need to consider when implementing standards-based grading.

1. Creating an implementation team

2. Establishing a common purpose of grading

3. Creating a multiyear professional learning plan for staff

4. Developing a master schedule that allows for remediation and enrichment

5. Anticipating common standards-based grading implementation roadblocks

These criteria are important as a team both begins and sustains the school's standards-based grading journey. As teams and teachers begin to implement standards-based grading in their classrooms, these criteria create the clarity and consistency that are needed across the school or district.

In other situations, we've seen district administrators mandate that standards-based grading be implemented within a certain time frame, which does not allow an implementation team to successfully respond to the needs of teachers. It's important to avoid this outcome because to sustain standards-based grading over time requires teacher voices working to enable and sustain professional learning that is differentiated and geared toward fidelity of implementation (Townsley, Buckmiller, & Cooper, 2019). Therefore, the purpose of this chapter is to describe how teacher leaders and administrators in a PLC should collaborate to implement standards-based grading across a school or district.

Unlike in previous chapters, where we included one PLC Connection section to address each standards-based grading principle, here we include a separate PLC Connection section for each criterion, with the exception of creating an implementation team. This is because we believe only a school principal or district superintendent are vested with the authority to create this team. While the voices of teachers are a necessary component of the implementation team, the *formation* of the team falls on the shoulders of school or district administrators. In addition, this chapter provides a standards-based grading continuum for implementation and an action-plan template to help readers determine the next steps in their implementation planning.

Creating an Implementation Team

School and district leaders may be tempted to take on the planning, communication, and professional learning associated with implementation without strong input from classroom teachers. Although such leaders are crucial for initiating and driving this effort, in highly effective schools, particularly those that are PLCs, collaborative goal setting that involves key stakeholders is the norm (Marzano & Waters, 2009). This chapter assumes that schools implementing standards-based grading in a PLC have a teaming structure in place for making these types of collaborative decisions. For example, some schools utilize an existing building leadership team, which is composed of administrators and a representative group of teachers. Other schools form a specific standards-based grading implementation team specifically for this purpose, which is the course we most recommend.

While some schools choose to include students or parents in the process, the leadership or implementation team should, at a minimum, comprise multiple teachers and administrators with policy and planning authority. It should also include those teachers in the school with strong interest or experience in standards-based grading in order to accelerate the learning curve of the entire implementation team. This team's goal is to support the school or district's vision of consistently implementing standards-based grading principles in a way that makes the most sense for the local community. If such a team is not yet in place at the school or district level, this team must be in place before the steps of implementation can occur.

After a team of teacher leaders and administrators is established (going forward, we refer to this as an *implementation team*), the team should work to understand the criteria for implementing standards-based grading we provide in this chapter.

Establishing a Common Purpose of Grading

The primary factors teachers consider when grading in a traditional way often include student effort, work habits, and academic performance (McMillan, 2001; McMillan et al., 2002). However, in standards-based grading, the purpose of grading is to communicate students' current levels of learning. To achieve this, the first step an implementation team should take when planning to implement standards-based grading is establishing their standards-based grading guidelines—that is, establishing a common purpose of grading that fits the unique culture and needs of the school, district, and community. Permitting individual teachers or even teams of teachers within a PLC to establish their own grading policies creates inequity for students across classrooms and grade levels. Furthermore, it may create frustration among parents who want the best for their learners and come to view standards-based grading is inhibiting learning due to inconsistent implementation (Webber Alder, 2019).

Many schools that implement standards-based grading begin by reading books and articles from authors who challenge the status quo of grading practices, such as Thomas R. Guskey (2015a), Ken O'Connor (2018), Rick Wormeli (2011), and Tom Schimmer (2016; Schimmer et al., 2018). These are all good places to start exploring ideas, but the work of implementation remains. Following a discussion of these ideas, the implementation team should develop a common set of grading guidelines. The three standards-based grading principles from this book are a solid starting point to expand on.

1. Grades should communicate students' current levels of learning based on standards.

2. Homework should serve as ungraded practice.

3. Students should have multiple opportunities to demonstrate their learning.

As an example of using this foundation to develop a common purpose, Des Moines Public Schools, whose vision is to become a model for urban education in the United States, has established five grading guidelines districtwide (see figure 5.1). You will find additional examples of standards-based grading guidelines in appendix B (page 157).

Des Moines Public Schools commits to all stakeholders to provide fair, accurate, specific, and timely information regarding student progress toward agreed-on common standards as well as feedback for next steps and growth areas. Grades communicate what students know and can do.

1. A consistent four-point grading scale is used.

2. Academic achievement is reported separately from behaviors.

3. Scores are based on a body of evidence.

4. Achievement is organized and reported by learning topic. In secondary schools, topic scores are converted to a grade at semester's end.

5. Students have multiple opportunities to demonstrate proficiency. Accommodations and modifications are provided for exceptional learners.

Source: © 2015 by Des Moines Public Schools.

Figure 5.1: Sample standards-based grading guidelines.

Des Moines Public Schools' priorities include an emphasis on grading in secondary schools because grades and grade point averages are needed for college and university transcripts. You'll notice how the guidelines in figure 5.1 emphasize that stakeholders should provide special attention to secondary schools. These guidelines state that administrators and teacher leaders should convert current levels of learning, based on standards communicated in the gradebook, to a grade at the end of the reporting period. The specifics of this conversion are emblematic of the kind of questions implementation teams must not overlook when establishing a common purpose for grading. In this case, a team must ask itself, "How can we fairly go about this?"

High schools might be tempted to convert current levels of learning to grades using a typical electronic gradebook that converts integers to percentages and then to a letter grade. Consider the sample electronic gradebook in figure 5.2.

Standard	Score
DNA and structure of proteins	2
Investigation of homeostasis	3
Models of cellular division	3
Models of cellular respiration	3
Models of photosynthesis	4
Key: 0 = No evidence of learning 1 = Minimal understanding 2 = Partial understanding 3 = Proficiency with standards 4 = Mastery of standards	

Figure 5.2: Sample end-of-reporting-period levels of understanding based on standards.

Figure 5.2 reports five standards using a five-level scale; therefore, there are a total of twenty standard points. By counting up the numbers in the second column, the student has a total of fifteen points based on his or her level of understanding. Fifteen divided by twenty equals 75 percent; therefore, the student earns a C based on a typical conversion scale from percentages to letter grades, in which 90 percent or better is an A, 80 to 89 percent is a B, 70 to 79 percent is a C, 60 to 69 percent is a D, and 59 percent or lower is an F.

Although the integers-to-percentages conversion method may be the easiest to implement using an electronic gradebook, and likely the simplest to understand for parents and students, the result still becomes points oriented. Does a student who showed proficiency or mastery in four out of five standards deserve a C? Similarly, if a student has a single 1 or 2, as in this case, it becomes easy to overlook when it's lumped into a series of proficient-or-better assessments as part of a final mathematical conversion.

Another method for determining letter grades based on current levels of learning in the gradebook is to use a logic rule. A *logic rule* is a "series of statements that describe how grades for standards will be converted into subject grades" (O'Connor, 2018, p. 191). A sample list of logic rules is as follows.

> *At the end of the reporting period:*
> - *Students must have all 4s in the gradebook to earn an A*
> - *Students must have 3s and 4s in the gradebook, with no more than one 2, to earn a B (no 0s or 1s)*
> - *Students must have no more than 50 percent of their marks be 2s, with the remaining marks being 3s or 4s, in the gradebook to earn a C (no 1s)*
> - *Students must have all 2s or 3s in the gradebook, with no more than one 1, to earn a D (no 0s)*
> - *Students with any 0s or more than one 1 in the gradebook earn an F*

Using this logic rule, the student in figure 5.2 (page 107), who has one 2, three 3s, and one 4, earns a B. If the student had a second 2 on a standard, the grade would fall to a C. A more thorough list of rules could account for what constitutes a plus or minus for a letter grade. Although few, if any, electronic gradebooks include logic rules in their features, an implementation team may favor this method because it offers teachers a fairer formula to assign grades. It also feels less based on adding up points than on encouraging students to improve on their lowest marks to improve their overall grade.

Ultimately, teams of teachers unified around a common purpose of grading will be able to more easily agree upon a method for determining letter grades. Because secondary teachers and students are incredibly in tune with GPAs, honor rolls, and valedictorians, agreeing on the purpose of grades and the methods for determining letter grades will go hand in hand.

PLC Connection

Parry Graham and William M. Ferriter (2010) suggest that the core leadership team in a PLC must commit to the same vision that it will filter to other teams. This idea holds true for an implementation team when developing standards-based grading guidelines. The team tasked with identifying and setting the school or district's grading guidelines must develop a common purpose that everyone in the school or district will follow. To do this, the implementation team should include teacher leaders among its members. Here's why: increasing teacher voice during multiple phases of standards-based grading implementation increases buy-in from all the staff

(Brookhart, 2011; Hill, 2018). Although administrators still have the authority and should be held responsible for the building's grading guidelines, including teacher input should be non-negotiable. Together, this team should explore grading research and best practices to come up with a unique set of guidelines. This section provides an implementation team with practical steps for establishing a common purpose of grading and grading guidelines.

Rather than starting with a discussion about grading scales, which electronic grade-book to use, or the format of the report card, an implementation team should begin by reading about the purpose of grading. Research-based literature contributing to the purpose of grading is outside the scope of this book, so we recommend leadership teams start by reading texts such as *How to Grade for Learning* (O'Connor, 2018), *On Your Mark* (Guskey, 2015a), *FAST Grading* (Reeves, 2016), and *Rethinking Grading* (Vatterott, 2015). Through reading these books, members of the implementation team should write their top three to five guidelines about the purpose of grading. Themes of communicating student learning, removing behaviors from the gradebook, and allowing reassessment opportunities are common themes in the research-based literature. In small groups, all members should indicate whether they agree or they disagree with each grading statement that other members have brainstormed. When a disagreement occurs, team members should be encouraged to share their opinions and suggest page references from the book (or books) they recently read supporting their perspectives. Use a template such as the one in figure 5.3 (page 110) to facilitate this process.

If one or more members of the implementation team have already started using standards-based grading practices, invite them to share their personal experiences related to the draft grading statements. Some schools may choose to invite teachers from another building or district to serve in this experience-sharing capacity. Following discussion at the team level about the pros and cons of each member's grading statements, the team should combine the ideas into a list of three to six grading guidelines that most members agree on.

Figure 5.4 (page 111) provides a tool teams can use to build consensus around the most important grading guidelines. Each implementation team member should first create a list of his or her preferred grading guidelines. Next, each team member passes his or her list to another team member who indicates his or her level of agreement by circling that level (disagree, unsure, or agree) next to each guideline. Each team member should rate each other's grading guidelines and then consider the most agreed-on statements as a starting point to consider in his or her classroom.

I believe the purpose of grades is . . .

Support for my purpose statement can be found . . .

Three guidelines about grading that are supported by research are . . .

Support for the first statement can be found . . .

Support for the second statement can be found . . .

Support for the third statement can be found . . .

Figure 5.3: My current beliefs about grading.

Visit **go.SolutionTree.com/PLCbooks** *for a free reproducible version of this figure.*

See appendix B (page 157) for several sample lists of building and district standards-based grading guidelines.

Creating a Multiyear Professional Learning Plan for Staff

Once a district or building establishes a common purpose of grading through an agreed-on set of grading guidelines, the next step for the implementation team is to create a multiyear professional learning plan for staff. Schools and districts commonly make the mistake of rushing implementation without giving proper weight for the need to prepare teachers to effectively use a standards-based grading system, which causes problems even when teachers are on board with the idea of standards-based grading (Johnston, 2018). Some of the earliest adopting secondary schools in Iowa attempted implementation using short timelines of one to three years. They found varying degrees of success. Since that time, educational researchers suggest that appropriate time to revise long-held beliefs about grading and assessment, coupled with adequate professional learning to understand the technical aspects of this change,

Directions: Choose your list of preferred grading statements, and then pass this page to each team member to choose (circle) his or her level of agreement with this statement. For larger teams, use multiple copies of this page.

Name:	Team Member: (circle one)	Team Member: (circle one)	Team Member: (circle one)	Team Member: (circle one)	Team Member: (circle one)
Grading statement:	Disagree Unsure Agree	Disagree Unsure Agree	Disagree Unsure Agree	Disagree Unsure Agree	Disagree Unsure Agree
Grading statement:	Disagree Unsure Agree	Disagree Unsure Agree	Disagree Unsure Agree	Disagree Unsure Agree	Disagree Unsure Agree
Grading statement:	Disagree Unsure Agree	Disagree Unsure Agree	Disagree Unsure Agree	Disagree Unsure Agree	Disagree Unsure Agree

Figure 5.4: Standards-based grading needs-assessment tool.

Visit go.SolutionTree.com/PLCbooks for a free reproducible version of this figure.

demand a more thoughtful approach of going slow early to go fast later (Townsley et al., 2019).

Following several years of several teachers' trying out standards-based grading principles in their own classrooms (which we elaborate on next), the Solon Community School District spent another year requiring secondary teachers to read and discuss a number of grading articles during professional learning time. After the board of education approved the district grading guidelines (the district's common purpose for grading), school leaders in Solon established a three-year implementation plan to phase in those guidelines. (Appendix B, page 157, includes a copy of these grading guidelines.)

In the first year, all secondary teachers engaged in professional learning about each grading guideline to understand what it meant, what it did not mean, how to implement it, and common pitfalls to avoid. During the second year, teachers were required to try out the grading guidelines in at least one unit of study and then go to school leaders with questions. The district provided follow-up professional learning in the second year to answer common questions and to support continued understanding and implementation of the grading guidelines. In the third year, teachers were required to fully implement the grading guidelines in all their courses, and the school's implementation team encouraged them to continue bringing their questions.

The specifics of a building or district's implementation plan will inevitably vary based on teachers' familiarity with standards-based grading principles; their experiences teaching and assessing the state, provincial, or national standards; and the time available for teachers' professional learning. Based on our experience working with secondary schools implementing standards-based grading, well-thought-out implementation plans require three years at minimum to fully establish, with four to five years being more common. PLCs with a strong understanding of the first critical question (What is it we want our students to learn?) are often able to accelerate the process because their teachers have a strong understanding of the standards. In addition, schools with teachers who have been piloting standards-based grading for several years are well-positioned to scale their implementation efforts more quickly through the use of internal staff leading professional learning rather than relying on external experts.

Regardless of these factors, the implementation team should consider collecting regular feedback from teacher teams regarding their implementation successes, hurdles, and concerns. We suggest a more formal process for creating and using these feedback loops in the next section.

PLC Connection

Although the implementation team should create a multiyear standards-based grading professional learning plan for staff, members should do this work in collaboration with the school or district leadership team. The district plan for professional learning should support the goals of the school implementation team in such a way that multiple initiatives are not competing for teachers' precious professional learning time in a given year. Here's why: while a few leaders may understand the building's long-term needs, a leadership team functioning within a PLC is best equipped to dig deep into the nuances of a personalized professional learning plan.

Teachers who have previously implemented standards-based grading report that staff will need a significant amount of professional learning time that is differentiated and flexible (Schiffman, 2016; Urich, 2012). Some teachers may have previous experience with standards-based grading or beliefs that strongly align with standards-based grading principles, while others may not be as familiar with the ideas. In addition, state, provincial, and national content standards are sometimes written in different ways, which may add to the complexity of implementing student- and parent-friendly standards for instruction, assessment, and gradebooks. The purpose of this section is to provide implementation teams with practical steps they can take to create a multiyear professional learning plan for teachers implementing standards-based grading.

After the implementation team has agreed on a common purpose of grading by creating a series of grading principles, the team's next step is to create a multiyear professional learning plan. This multiyear plan will help teachers better understand the supports and corresponding timeline that they will receive. In addition, this plan can clarify the change process for all educators in the PLC. Implementation teams should consider three important questions when developing their professional learning plans.

1. By the end of the year, what steps toward standards-based grading do we want to accomplish together? (Goals)

2. At the end of the year, what artifacts can we collect to document progress toward our goal? (Evidence)

3. How will we determine our progress along the way? (Monitoring)

These three questions align with the three big ideas of a PLC (a focus on learning, a collaborative culture, and a results orientation; DuFour et al., 2016). Each of these questions and their resulting actions can only be accomplished when a collaborative culture is evident and the teams focus on learning about their progress as educators. Because a PLC strives to demonstrate a results orientation, implementation teams should set annual goals, determine reasonable evidence that they can collect to demonstrate progress toward the goals, and monitor progress along the way. Prior to setting goals for the first year of implementation, implementation teams might collect teacher perceptions of the grading guidelines using a needs assessment, such as the one in figure 5.5.

Directions: Our building is on a multiyear journey to implementing standards-based grading. To personalize our professional learning for the upcoming school year, it is important for the grading leadership team to understand the staff's current thinking about grading. Please respond to the following questions and statements.

Grading principle: Grades should communicate students' current levels of learning based on standards.
What reservations, if any, do you have about implementing this grading principle?

What questions do you have about implementing this grading principle in your classroom?

Circle the phrase that best describes your current thinking about this grading guideline:

Looking for more support   **Not sure yet**   **Ready to try it**

Grading principle: Homework should serve as ungraded practice.
What reservations, if any, do you have about implementing this grading principle?

What questions do you have about implementing this grading principle in your classroom?

Circle the phrase that best describes your current thinking about this grading guideline:

Looking for more support   **Not sure yet**   **Ready to try it**

Grading principle: Students should have multiple opportunities to demonstrate their learning.

What reservations, if any, do you have about implementing this grading principle?

What questions do you have about implementing this grading principle in your classroom?

Circle the phrase that best describes your current thinking about this grading guideline:

Looking for more support   **Not sure yet**   **Ready to try it**

Figure 5.5: Standards-based grading needs assessment.

Visit ***go.SolutionTree.com/PLCbooks*** *for a free reproducible version of this figure.*

Using the results from this survey, the implementation team should establish one or more goals for the upcoming school year. For example, a school with a majority of teachers who are *not sure yet* about providing multiple opportunities for students to demonstrate understanding might establish this goal: *By the end of the school year, over 50 percent of our teachers will rate themselves as* ready to try it *for the third grading principle on the assessment survey.*

After establishing a goal, the implementation team should consider what evidence it can collect to determine progress toward its goal. In the case of the preceding goal, each team of teachers could develop and deploy a unified reassessment policy through collaborative work. (See chapter 4's PLC Connection on page 88 for details on this process.) The implementation team would then collect the team-developed reassessment policies along with a reflection from each team on the successes and struggles the teams have experienced using the policy. At the end of the school year, the implementation team should ask all teachers to complete the standards-based grading needs assessment tool (figure 5.4, page 111) to see what progress, if any, teachers have made toward this goal.

Note that the implementation team should not wait until the end of the year to check on the status of its goal, which is why it collects the team-developed reassessment policies and reflections during the year. As the old adage goes, "What gets monitored gets done"; having teams establish reassessment policies and share subsequent reflections requires that the teams plan ahead to monitor the goal.

Oftentimes, the most effective monitoring involves feedback loops with teams in a PLC. For example, once per month, the implementation team might ask leaders from each teacher team to share a current success and struggle stemming from their team's reassessment policy by writing it on a sticky note. The implementation team should review this information, summarize any themes, and respond to any collective concerns via a schoolwide clarifying communication or by suggesting next steps at an upcoming professional learning day. Through establishing and following up on these feedback loops, the implementation team validates and responds to staff concerns early in the process, rather than waiting until the end of the year.

In summary, an implementation team should set annual goals, determine reasonable evidence that it can collect to demonstrate progress toward the goals, and monitor progress along the way. Figure 5.6 shows an example of a goal-setting worksheet based on a school implementing a standards-based grading system.

Goal	Evidence	Monitoring
By the end of the school year, over 50 percent of our teachers will rate themselves as ready to try it for the third grading principle on the assessment survey.	Collect team-developed reassessment policies annually with a reflection on current successes and struggles. Collect results from the end-of-year standards-based grading needs assessment.	Leaders from each teacher team will share a current success and struggle stemming from their team's reassessment policy by writing it on a sticky note. The sticky notes will be read at each grading leadership team meeting. A member of the grading leadership team will provide follow-up for each sticky note.

Figure 5.6: Standards-based grading annual goal-setting worksheet.

*Visit **go.SolutionTree.com/PLCbooks** for a free reproducible version of this figure.*

After it establishes the goals, evidence, and feedback loops for the upcoming school year, the implementation team should consider drafting goals for one or more additional years. For example, a school might set goals during a three-year period, as in figure 5.7. Through this multiyear plan, teachers can review and understand the supports and corresponding timeline they will receive.

Year	Focus Area	Goal	Evidence	Monitoring
2019–2020	Standards-based grading principle 3	By the end of the school year, over 50 percent of our teachers will rate themselves as ready to try it for the third grading principle on the assessment survey.	Midyear and end-of-year survey results are summarized and shared with the implementation team as well as all staff. At least ten teachers have shared out their third grading principle implementation plans during a faculty meeting.	The implementation team will conduct midyear and end-of-year surveys. The implementation team will add a related agenda item each quarter to check in on this goal.
2020–2021	Standards-based grading principle 2	By the end of the school year, we will no longer assign a point value for homework in the gradebook.	Each teacher will print out electronic gradebook summaries for anonymous students and share them at their collaborative team meetings.	The principal will randomly check at least one class gradebook for each teacher one month into each reporting period.
2021–2022	Standards-based grading principles 1–3	By the end of the school year, over 90 percent of our teachers will rate themselves as ready to try it for all three grading principles on the assessment survey.	Midyear and end-of-year survey results are summarized and shared with the implementation team as well as all staff. At least twenty teachers have shared out their grading principle implementation plans during a faculty meeting.	The implementation team will conduct midyear and end-of-year surveys. The implementation team will add a related agenda item each quarter to checkin on this goal.

Figure 5.7: Multiyear standards-based grading implementation timeline.

*Visit **go.SolutionTree.com/PLCbooks** for a free reproducible version of this figure.*

Draft this plan in pencil. As teacher teams continue to provide their successes and hurdles through the feedback loops designed to monitor each annual goal, the implementation team may determine goals that need to be amended, accelerated, or even curtailed. Following the completion of a draft multiyear professional learning plan, the grading leadership team can communicate its vision for implementing standards-based grading. Because teams in a PLC focus on results (DuFour et al., 2008; DuFour et al., 2016), it is important to establish, support, and monitor goals through a multiyear professional learning plan.

Developing a Master Schedule That Allows for Remediation and Enrichment

The implementation team will need to work with all connected stakeholders, such as teacher leaders and administrators, to change the master schedule to support remediation and enrichment. They must build this time into the master schedule during the school day. Without this important block of time, teachers will be unable to provide standards-specific remediation for students who need additional instruction or enrichment for those already showing mastery of learning standards. Each teacher's relearning plan should clarify what this additional instruction looks like for students who have not yet demonstrated understanding. See chapter 4 (page 71) for additional details.

Before we address the issues of time (how long to devote to the process of remediation and enrichment), focus first on your existing master schedule. When examining your master schedule, you may find you need to create time that doesn't exist within the schedule, as in figure 5.8, which depicts a sample sixth-grade schedule. In this example, this middle school created flextime between class periods (mods). Your school can accomplish a similar structure by working within the parameters of your daily schedule to adjust class time, passing time, and other factors so you create additional periods. Also, notice in this sample how the school included two blocks, flextime and WOW (working on work) time, that it added to allow for reteaching and reassessments during the school day. In this case, flextime is a specific block where teachers can request students for reassessments, while WOW is equivalent to a study hall but can also be used for reteaching and reassessment.

The most important takeaway from figure 5.8 is that it creates time on the master schedule to allow for reteaching and reassessment to support students who have not yet demonstrated understanding as well as for those in need of enrichment. How your school arranges this time for the school day is variable; what matters is that this time exists, and it doesn't have to come out of thin air.

The implementation team can repurpose existing time within the master schedule to allow for remediation and enrichment. To illustrate this, let's bring back an

Teacher	Mod 1 (8:15–9:01 a.m.)	Mod 2 (9:05–9:51 a.m.)	Mod 3 (9:55–10:41 a.m.)	Flex and lunch (10:45–11:32 a.m.)
Jackson	Reading	Prep	Reading	Flex
Raju	Prealgebra	Prep	Mathematics	Flex
Mooney	Science	Prep	Science	Flex
MacLennan	Social studies	Prep	Prep	Flex
Hirway	English language arts	Prep	Prep	Flex

Teacher	Mod 4 (11:37 a.m.–12:33 p.m.)	Mod 5 (12:38–1:24 p.m.)	Mod 6 (1:29–2:15 p.m.)	Mod 7 (2:20–2:40 p.m.)	Mod 8 (2:45–3:31 p.m.)
Jackson	Prep	Reading	Reading	WOW	Reading
Raju	Mathematics	Prep	Mathematics	WOW	Mathematics
Mooney	Science	Science	Prep	WOW	Science
MacLennan	Social studies	Social studies	Social studies	WOW	Social studies
Hirway	English language arts	English language arts	English language arts	WOW	English language arts

Figure 5.8: Master schedule using flextime.

example from chapter 4 (page 83). In figure 5.9, the high school repurposed an ineffective homeroom and advisory time, called *seminar*, and focused on using that time to instead provide remediation and enrichment. Students that were proficient in standards used this time to attend optional club meetings, music practices, extra recreation time for physical education, or as an open study hall period. Teachers requested students on certain days of the week, and staff assigned students to rooms based on individual student needs.

Regular Day		
	Start Time	End Time
First Block	8:20 a.m.	9:44 a.m.
Second Block	9:49 a.m.	11:13 a.m.
Lunch or Seminar	11:16 a.m.	11:46 a.m.
Lunch or Seminar	11:48 a.m.	12:18 p.m.
Third Block	12:22 p.m.	1:46 p.m.
Fourth Block	1:51 p.m.	3:15 p.m.

Figure 5.9: Master schedule using advisory time.

Ultimately, creating time for remediation and enrichment is about the implementation team working to identify two items: (1) the appropriate amount of time and (2) the appropriate placement in the day. Most schools will find that twenty to thirty minutes is an appropriate amount of time for this work. The school we know that used the schedule in figure 5.9 (page 119) chose to build this period into the middle part of the day so students participating in extracurriculars at the end of the day could continue with those activities while still being available for remediation and enrichment. Note that it took longer than a single academic year to develop and implement the schedules in figure 5.8 (page 119) and figure 5.9, so the details you see in these examples reflect multiple trials and refinements based on teacher input over multiple years.

PLC Connection

Having time for remediation and enrichment in the master schedule further supports the work of a PLC because, when teams begin to determine how to collectively respond when students have not yet learned curricula content and how to extend and enrich the learning for those students who have demonstrated proficiency (PLC critical questions 3 and 4), they will realize that regular class time cannot effectively serve all students. Some students will need additional time and support, which a school can only offer through changes to the master schedule. After the schedule is established, teacher teams can work on developing priority days for certain content areas to provide remediation and enrichment.

Imagine a student who is struggling in multiple content areas. This student may receive requests from multiple teachers throughout the week to attend a remediation session. Therefore, departmental teacher teams should work with the other departmental teams to identify specific days where a specific team or content area takes priority. Ultimately, the building administrator provides oversight to ensure a schedule that works across the building, which includes prioritizing different content areas based on the building's academic profile and student learning needs. Within departmental teams, individual teachers can then collaborate to plan remediation activities, share students between teachers, provide study sessions, or collaborate around standards-specific learning targets.

For example, mathematics and social studies teachers may have priority for scheduling students on Tuesday and Thursday while science, language arts, and other content areas may have priority for scheduling students the remaining days of the week. In essence, a master schedule that supports remediation further supports the PLC process in and across the departments within the school. Building administrators will need to weigh in as they seek a results orientation for their PLC and its quest toward ensuring all students learn at high levels.

Anticipating Common Standards-Based Grading Implementation Roadblocks

Schools may experience a number of roadblocks when implementing standards-based grading, some of which may come from parents (Holland, 2018; Peters & Buckmiller, 2014; Webber Alder, 2019). Before educators implement a standards-based grading system, it is important that they understand the assumptions and beliefs parents hold regarding education and grading. At Solon High School, it took us several meetings and discussions with parents throughout the initial phase of our implementation to understand common themes. These assumptions and beliefs often trump rational thought and can easily become divisive roadblocks if educators don't know about and plan for them. Although parents may have beliefs about school that are local to your context, there are some common assumptions that most parents make about standards-based grading. The following sections will help guide you through three common issues that may come up with parents when you begin implementation: (1) the language of grades, (2) implications for college and university admissions, and (3) loss of control of the points game. We close with a final PLC Connection about how teams can work collaboratively to anticipate and manage roadblocks, including issues that come up outside of parent concerns.

The Language of Grades

Parents assume they know what letter grades mean. Growing up, most modern adults received a series of A–F grades on each report card. Most everyone who experienced some type of formal schooling understands what it means to fail as well as what it means to get an A. But ask a group of parents to describe what a B, C, or D mean, and you are bound to get diverse responses.

As we have explored in this book, grades are *not* a common language for educators either. Educators have included so many factors in letter grades that result in grades often varying significantly from teacher to teacher. Look at the information in figure 5.10 (page 122). What does it tell you about the variability in traditional grading? Which student listed here has shown he or she has mastered the most learning standards? Which grading method is the fairest? Which makes the most sense?

Student	Task 1	Task 2	Task 3	Task 4	Task 5	Average Score and Final Grade	Median Score and Final Grade	Average Score With Lowest Grade Deleted and Final Grade
Troy Arendt	40%	100%	95%	98%	45%	76% (C)	95% (A)	85% (B)
Nina O'Brien	70%	87%	88%	76%	74%	79% (C)	76% (C)	81% (B)
Lizzie Begnaud	90%	94%	89%	74%	48%	79% (C)	89% (B)	87% (B)
Genny Jackson	0%	95%	98%	95%	100%	78% (C)	95% (A)	97% (A)
Peter Mensching	55%	68%	89%	79%	100%	78% (C)	79% (C)	84% (B)
Luis Fernandez	90%	90%	42%	80%	97%	80% (B)	90% (A)	89% (B)

Source: Adapted from Guskey, 2002.

Figure 5.10: Results of various grading methods.

Although it ultimately provides a common purpose and understanding of grading, standards-based grading changes the common language parents have traditionally relied on to communicate with teachers. As a result, parents have to ask different questions to interpret their child's grade. This change can make parents nervous because they don't know the language to use to support their child in a standards-based grading setting. For example, think about this list of questions that parents traditionally ask their children. Notice the common language focuses on *behaviors* and *actions*.

- "What can you do to raise your grade?"

- "When will the next extra credit be offered?"

- "Did you get your homework done?"

- "Why did you miss points on this homework assignment?"

- "When are you going to turn in that missing assignment?"

To help parents understand this new common language in a standards-based system, we have to teach them to ask new questions. This list shows questions teachers should encourage parents to ask in a standards-based system. Notice the common language focuses on *learning*, *standards*, and *assessment*.

- "What standards do you think you still need to learn?"

- "When was the last time you practiced or worked on _____?"

- "When was the last time you were assessed on _____?"

- "When is your next opportunity to reassess on _____?"

- "What practice, studying, or reteaching opportunities have you completed in preparation for the next reassessment opportunity?"

When implementing standards-based grading, the implementation team should provide the necessary information and guidance teachers need to retrain parents to ask these questions with a focus on learning, standards, and assessment rather than behaviors and actions. One way to do this is to provide teachers with a cheat sheet of common questions parents might ask their children and how to reframe them for a standards-based mindset. Figure 5.11 (page 124) compares questions that parents are used to asking with questions teachers and schools should encourage them to ask instead.

Questions parents often ask students in a traditional grading system	Recommended questions for parents to ask in a standards-based grading system
"What can you do to raise your grade right now?"	"What standards do you think you still need to learn or improve at?"
"When will the next extra credit be offered?"	"When is your next opportunity to reassess on _____?"
"Did you get your homework done?"	"What is the standard you are practicing tonight, and how well are you practicing it?"

Figure 5.11: Sample guidance for helping parents ask standards-based grading questions.

Implications for College and University Admissions

Historically, the higher-education admissions process has required potential students to report their college entrance exam score (or scores), courses completed, and grade point average in their applications. However, colleges and universities are increasingly dropping SAT and ACT requirements (Jaschik, 2018). When college entrance exam scores are no longer reported, the remaining reported criteria automatically increase in importance. Therefore, a strong grade point average aligned with course standards is important for students. In Iowa, for example, public universities use an admissions index, which takes into account class rank, grade point average, and college entrance exam score (Board of Regents, State of Iowa, n.d.). If a student does not have one or more of these measures, then an admissions office administrator must review transcripts to determine an admittance decision. So, it comes as no surprise that parents of high school students who are applying to these schools are paying even more attention to letter grades and grade point averages.

Given this, parents and guardians may wonder how changing to standards-based grading at the high school level will impact their child's chances of being admitted to a university. Even if parents are familiar with standards-based grading at the elementary or middle school level, in which standards are not converted to letter grades, they may wonder how college admissions offices will view a no-grades high school transcript. To calm these fears of the unfamiliar, high schools using standards-based grading should communicate to parents their practice of converting gradebook information to letter grades and those letter grades to grade point averages at the end of the reporting period. We also advise that school leaders point out the research from Buckmiller and Peters

(2018) in which they interview multiple admissions offices and find that, once standards-based grading principles are explained to admissions directors, university officials express general approval of standards-based grading systems. While letter grades and grade point averages are clearly norms on high school transcripts, admissions offices were receptive to alternatives, which currently exist in very small cases across the United States. Finally, this research concludes admissions personnel have placed a tremendous amount of trust in grades and college admissions scores due to their efficiency and limited resources to make these important decisions (Buckmiller & Peters, 2018). Similarly, the New England Secondary School Consortium (n.d.) has gathered the perspectives of sixty-eight colleges and universities, stating students with proficiency-based transcripts will not be at a disadvantage during the admissions process.

High school leaders considering standards-based grading should proactively communicate to parents not only what will be changing, such as the look of the gradebook and the point value of homework, but also what will not be changing—the use of letter grades and grade point averages. Parents may make some assumptions based on what they have read online or previously experienced; therefore, it is important to anticipate these common concerns by sharing information related to standards-based grading and the college and university admissions process. Figure 5.12 (page 126) depicts a cheat sheet of examples of some of the most common parent assumptions about standards-based grading and potential school responses.

Loss of Control of the Points Game

From birth, parents nurture and develop children by modeling, explaining, and teaching through all of life's events. Parents naturally fall into the role of teacher by holding the information and sharing that information at appropriate times. Parenting is a natural way of expressing the idea, "I know more than you." Think of all the times you asked your parents for something, and their response was, "Because I said so." One of the challenges for parents and their children during adolescent years ultimately comes down to adjusting to the rapidly changing power structure between them. It's not uncommon for this dynamic to also play out in our schools. Grading practices have a part to play in both of these.

Put simply, standards-based grading gives students more power, which, in turn, can make teachers nervous, because they can no longer use points to direct students. Teachers are no longer the sole provider of points as students become more empowered to improve their gradebooks and report cards by showing they have mastered learning standards at a higher level.

Common Parent Assumption	Potential School Response
"There is going to be a dip in my student's understanding of this new system that will negatively impact his or her grade point average."	"The school will continue to assess and monitor student achievement and grade point average. There is no reason for the grade point average to change as we still determine a final letter grade."
"Admissions offices at colleges and universities aren't going to understand the changes in grading, and it will put my student at a disadvantage."	"Research demonstrates that college admissions offices are already aware of significant differences in grading practices from school to school based on the research. We will still report a grade point average that reflects a student's cumulative knowledge of high school courses."
"My student will miss out on scholarship opportunities because you are changing the way you grade."	"Students will continue to receive scholarship opportunities based on the grade point average they earn as well as based on their overall achievement in high school."

Figure 5.12: Common parent assumptions about standards-based grading and school responses.

Just as it does with teachers, standards-based grading takes some power away from parents because it gives students more control over how and when they demonstrate their understanding (Knight & Cooper, 2019). For example, in the past, parents may have asked teachers for extra-credit opportunities on behalf of their students, but extra credit no longer exists with standards-based grading. However, students do have the power to approach their teachers about reassessment opportunities.

This loss of power can be extremely frustrating for parents who want to control every aspect of their child's schooling. In our experience, these parents may put up a lot of roadblocks by doing things like citing contradictory research studies on grading, clamoring for more time before changes are implemented, and demanding that schools hold on to past practices. Ultimately, these parental beliefs come down to power, and some parents do not want to relinquish a portion of that control to their children. Figure 5.13 offers a cheat sheet of several common parent questions related to power and potential school responses.

Common Parent Assumption	Potential School Response
"There is little to no research that supports standards-based grading."	"There is little to no research that supports the traditional grading system. In fact, many educational researchers have pointed out problems with the default grading system, while there is research to support the effectiveness of standards-based grading."
"My student does all the homework and should be rewarded for the effort of doing the work."	"We still want students to do homework, and the students who do will perform better on assessments. Strong understanding will always be rewarded."
"It would be better if you started using this system with next year's students."	"The work of grading and assessment is our main objective in school. It is important work and should not be delayed."
"Students who get an assessment right the first time deserve more credit than students who don't. Not everyone deserves an A."	"We have made it our mission for every student to be a successful learner by the conclusion of each course. Not all students learn at the same rate, but any student who shows mastery of learning standards at a course's conclusion deserves an A. More earned As reflect a job well done."

Figure 5.13: Common parent assumptions and school responses on power dynamics in grading.

PLC Connection

This set of sections documented several common roadblocks to consider when implementing standards-based grading. This is not an exhaustive list, and the specific concerns parents, teachers, and other stakeholders may raise are often contextual. For this PLC Connection, we will discuss a more formal process for considering and responding to roadblocks from various areas, including but not limited to parents.

As with the other aspects of implementing standards-based grading, a team working within a PLC can best anticipate common standards-based grading implementation roadblocks. Here's why: the power of a PLC is that of teacher collective efficacy (Donohoo, 2017; Voelkel & Chrispeels, 2017). While a teacher alone may be able to anticipate many of the barriers that will inevitably come up during the change process, more heads around the table equals more potential to consider roadblocks as well as solutions. Efficacious teams realize a team has greater influence than any one individual. Additionally, efficacious teams have protocols and processes in place to collaboratively find solutions. Therefore, teams need to develop a process to address concerns whenever a roadblock presents itself. To establish this process, teams of teachers in a PLC should consider the following questions when they encounter roadblocks with standards-based grading.

- Is this a team roadblock?

- Is this a student roadblock?

- Is this a curricular roadblock (such as availability of instructional materials, sequencing, pacing, or the rigor of standards)?

- Is this a roadblock with the assessment itself (such as its format or a prompt)?

- Is this a roadblock with an outside agent (such as parents, the community, or the board of education)?

Once the team has classified the roadblock (the team, student, curriculum, assessment, or outside agent), the team next discusses it and comes up with one or more action steps. Consider the following scenario. In a middle school classroom, one student approaches a teacher and says, "My friend in Mr. Brown's class gets to reassess after the unit test. Why aren't we allowed to do that in this class?" The teacher realizes not everyone on the team is currently providing students multiple opportunities to demonstrate understanding in a consistent manner—a student and team roadblock. The necessary action step is for the teacher to add *Review team reassessment policy* to the upcoming weekly meeting agenda.

During the meeting, once the team reviews its reassessment policy, the teacher shares her student's concern to help team members better understand the context of the roadblock. Each team member is then allowed to comment on whether the student's concern meets the agreed-on grading policy. If it does not meet the policy, the team decides if an exception is appropriate. If the team does not make an exception, it agrees to move forward in a consistent manner. The team's decision is then recorded in meeting minutes, and it selects a teacher to follow up with the student. In this particular case, the team ended up allowing the student a chance to demonstrate learning by taking another version of the test. As teams collect data on these cases, they should present these data to the principal whenever they believe there is evidence that a grading guideline needs revision. Figure 5.14 provides a template that teams can use to work through such standards-based grading implementation roadblocks.

Describe the roadblock:

What is this roadblock related to? (Circle one.)
    Our teacher team   A student   Curriculum
                    Assessment   An outside agent
What action steps does our team need to take right now related to this roadblock?

What is our agreed-on solution to this roadblock?

Figure 5.14: Team template for working through standards-based grading implementation roadblocks.

Visit go.SolutionTree.com/PLCbooks for a free reproducible version of this figure.

In some instances, a team of teachers in a PLC may not have adequate resources or authority to enact a solution. Sometimes, school administrators may need to enter the conversation. For example, a parent may have a concern that his or her middle school child will not be able to come in after school to complete several needed reassessments. A team of teachers may agree it would be best to create an intervention time at the end of the school day when teachers can work with students who need additional time and support outside the classroom. In this case, the principal must be involved, as the potential solution would require a change to the master schedule.

Early on in the standards-based grading implementation process, teams will need to share the roadblocks they are experiencing with the grading leadership team so that the team can add any common questions and solutions to a schoolwide FAQ or upcoming teacher professional development days.

Assessment Tools for Your Journey

The major purpose of this chapter is to describe how teacher leaders and administrators in a PLC collectively plan supports for implementing standards-based grading across an entire secondary building or district. Using figure 5.15, leadership or implementation teams should assess themselves along the continuum for implementing standards-based grading in a school or district. (See page 145 for a reproducible version of this continuum.) Leadership or implementation teams should use the reported levels of implementation of the grading criteria to plan follow-up implementation supports.

With figure 5.15 complete, use the action-plan template in figure 5.16 (page 132) to write down your school's current level of implementation and next steps. (See page 153 for a reproducible version of this action-plan template.)

Directions: As a team, circle each criterion that aligns with your team's current level of implementation of standards-based grading across the building. Consider the evidence following the criteria as examples of artifacts your team can provide or share with school or district leaders or administration. Note it is possible to circle some of the criteria in the implementing category while circling some of the criteria in the sustaining category.

Getting Started	Implementing	Sustaining
Criteria: The building has not yet developed a common purpose of grading.	**Criteria:** Grading guidelines have been established at the team level, but not schoolwide, in order to communicate the purpose of grading.	**Criteria:** The building leadership team has established schoolwide grading guidelines. A schoolwide process is in place to determine letter grades from standards.
Evidence: No grading purpose statements exist. Grading policies and procedures are individually developed by teachers. No standards-based grading professional learning plan has been developed.	**Evidence:** A team-developed grading purpose statement or grading guidelines exist. The building leadership team has developed a standards-based grading professional learning plan for the next semester or academic year and shared it with staff.	**Evidence:** The building leadership team has agreed on buildingwide grading guidelines and shared them with key stakeholders. The building leadership team has developed a multiyear standards-based grading professional learning plan and shared it with key stakeholders inside and outside the school.

The building leadership team has not discussed or considered changes to the master schedule supporting standards-based grading in a professional learning community. The leadership team has not discussed or considered possible standards-based grading implementation roadblocks. No leadership team agenda items or minutes document anticipated roadblocks.	The building leadership team has developed a master schedule change for the upcoming academic year. The leadership team has shared the updated master schedule for the next academic year with staff. The leadership team has discussed a few, but not all, possible standards-based grading implementation roadblocks. Notes from leadership team minutes document a few possible roadblocks.	The leadership team has tried out, evaluated, and revised a master schedule change to support remediation and enrichment opportunities for students. Leadership team minutes document discussion of the initial master schedule change and needed revisions. The leadership team has shared the revised master schedule with staff. The leadership team has extensively discussed possible standards-based grading implementation roadblocks and proactively communicated solutions with key stakeholders. The leadership team has shared a FAQ document with teachers and parents.

Figure 5.15: Continuum for implementing standards-based grading schoolwide or districtwide.

My team's current level on the continuum for implementing standards-based grading in a school or district is best described as (circle one):

Getting started   **Implementing**   **Sustaining**

Evidence my team can provide to support our current level includes:

Directions: Use the following table to plan your team's next steps.

Desired Level and Criteria: Where do we want to be?	Action: What do we need to do to move closer to sustaining on the standards-based grading continuum for schoolwide or districtwide implementation?	Change: What do we need to change or give up?	Evidence of Success: What products, policies, or procedures would demonstrate our desired criteria?

Figure 5.16: Action-plan template for implementation of standards-based grading schoolwide or districtwide.

Conclusion

This book provides the tools and processes for a secondary-level PLC to establish a standards-based grading system. Although the work is not always easy, when they see the impact on learning, many teachers we've worked with have found it to be the most rewarding work in their career. Think of the power that teams in a PLC have when implementing the standards-based grading principles outlined in this book. Students, with support from both teachers and parents, have the power to take control of their learning as the standards become impactful teaching tools, fostering a renewed focus on and commitment to learning. Through these principles, students have the power to reassess and practice additional learning in an environment that supports academic success. Teacher teams will have the power to look at assessment data together, analyze students' results, and target interventions to maximize the potential for improving students' learning.

The era of sorting students into bell-shaped curves based on achievement has passed. We need teachers who are willing to embrace the principles of PLCs to develop the talent of all students and not just sort it. You can be that teacher or leader who ensures that your school's grading practices emphasize the three big ideas of a PLC: (1) a focus on learning, (2) a collaborative culture, and (3) a results orientation (DuFour et al., 2016). The tools are within these pages. Make learning the constant for all students, and you will see amazing results.

Consider the example of the Granite School District in Salt Lake County, Utah, which reports that students are taking more ownership of their learning and teachers are excited to see their students succeed (Roe, 2019). Likewise, the Des Moines Public Schools standards-referenced grading system has created much more equitable learning outcomes for students across its urban district (Aguilar, 2019). Nothing is stopping your school from achieving this kind of success with its grading practices.

Think back to the story we shared in the introduction to this book (page 1) that compelled our school to move to standards-based grading practices. Two classrooms, two teachers, and two completely different assessment styles, and students asked (some might even describe it as *begged*) to be moved to a section that allowed standards-based grading practices. With your PLC as your foundation, you have the same power we did to rethink how your school or district grades its students and improve learning for all. We hope this book has provided the same incentive.

Jimmy Casas is the CEO and president of J Casas and Associates (https://jimmy casas.com), an educational leadership company aimed at serving teachers, principals, and superintendents in school districts across the United States. He once said to us that, when talking about a change initiative, the question you have to ask is, "What are you waiting for?" (J. Casas, personal communication, November 18, 2013). That question immediately made us spring into action. We knew that waiting for someone else or a better time to do this work was not in the best interest of our students. You have the tools to start implementing standards-based grading. So now we ask you, What are *you* waiting for?

Standards-Based Grading Implementation Continua and Action-Plan Templates

In this appendix, you will find full sets of the standards-based grading continua and action-plan templates featured in chapters 2–5 of this book, organized by the individual assessments, the team assessments, the continuum for implementing standards-based grading schoolwide or districtwide, and each of their associated action-plan templates. Visit **go.SolutionTree.com/PLCbooks** to download these reproducible tools.

Continuum for Standards-Based Grading Principle 1—Individual Assessment

Directions: As an individual, circle each criterion that aligns with your current level of implementation of the first standards-based grading principle—grades should communicate students' current levels of learning based on standards. Consider the evidence following the criteria as examples of artifacts you or other team members can provide or share with each other as well as other teams in your PLC. Note it is possible to circle criteria from multiple categories.

Getting Started	Implementing	Sustaining
Criteria: Numbers in the gradebook are based on assessment tasks. None of my standards are based on state, provincial, or national standards. I have not yet taken the time to look at the number of standards I teach in each course to see if it is manageable to assess and record them all. When I return an assessment to students, it usually includes one overall score.	**Criteria:** Some, but not all numbers in the gradebook are based on standards rather than assessment tasks. Most of my standards are based on state, provincial, or national standards. I have looked at the number of standards I assess and record in each course; however, I am not yet sure if my list is manageable. When I return an assessment to students, it includes a score for each standard assessed.	**Criteria:** All numbers in the gradebook are based on standards rather than assessment tasks. All my standards are based on state, provincial, or national standards. I regularly review the number of standards I assess and record in each course, and I believe my list is manageable for the most part. When I return an assessment to students, it includes a score for each standard assessed, and I have rewritten these standards in a way that students and parents can understand.

Getting Started	Implementing	Sustaining
Evidence: Gradebooks include assessment tasks such as homework, quizzes, tests, and projects. Course standards are not yet documented or reviewed. I am not aware of the number of standards I am assessing. Completed student assessments indicate one overall score.	**Evidence:** Gradebooks include a mix of assessment tasks such as homework, quizzes, tests, and projects, as well as number based upon standards. All numbers in the gradebook are based on standards. There is written or verbal articulation between course standards and state, provincial, or national standards. I have discomfort with the number of standards. Completed student assessments indicate point-based scores for each standard.	**Evidence:** All numbers in the gradebook are based on standards. There is written articulation between course standards and state, provincial, or national standards. I am comfortable with the number of standards. Completed student assessments indicate numbers, such as 1–4, based on the level of learning for each standard (which are written in a parent- and student-friendly way).

Continuum for Standards-Based Grading Principle 2—Individual Assessment

Directions: As an individual, circle each criterion that aligns with your current level of implementation of the second standards-based grading principle—homework should serve as ungraded practice. Consider the evidence following the criteria as examples of artifacts you or other team members can provide or share with each other as well as other teams in your PLC. Note it is possible to circle criteria from multiple categories.

Getting Started	Implementing	Sustaining
Criteria: Homework and independent practice are part of my students' final grade.	**Criteria:** Homework and practice assignments are not part of my students' final grade. Some students are able to articulate the role of homework and independent practice in my classes.	**Criteria:** Homework and practice assignments are not part of my students' final grade. Most students are able to articulate the role of homework and independent practice in my classes.
I give little feedback to my students.	My students receive feedback on some, but not all, of my homework and independent practice.	My students receive feedback on most of my homework and independent practice.
My homework and independent practice assignments do not have a clear connection to course standards.	Some, but not all, of my homework and independent practice assignments are purposeful and have a clear connection to course standards.	I can articulate the connection between all my homework and practice assignments and course standards as well as the purpose of each independent practice assignment.
I do not use homework and independent practice to guide instruction.	I occasionally address students who are not consistently completing homework and independent practice.	I regularly address students who are not consistently completing their homework and practice assignments, and I initiate contact with parents when a student is not completing the homework and independent practice.
	I sometimes use the results of homework and independent practice to guide instruction or provide interventions.	

Getting Started	Implementing	Sustaining
		I regularly use the results of homework and independent practice to guide instruction or provide interventions.
Evidence: My gradebook indicates homework and independent practice are part of students' final grade. My gradebook indicates that most students are not doing the homework and independent practice.	**Evidence:** Lesson plans indicate feedback opportunities (teacher, peer, textbook, online, and so on) for some homework and independent practice. I have examples of conversations with students who are not consistently completing homework and independent practice. My gradebook indicates that some students are completing homework and independent practice.	**Evidence:** Lesson plans indicate feedback opportunities (teacher, peer, textbook, online, and so on) for most homework and independent practice. I have a documented protocol I use to address students who are not consistently completing independent practice. I have multiple examples of conversations with students who are not consistently completing homework and independent practice. My gradebook indicates that the majority of students are completing homework and independent practice.

Continuum for Standards-Based Grading Principle 3—Individual Assessment

Directions: As an individual, circle each criterion that aligns with your current level of implementation of the third standards-based grading principle—students should have multiple opportunities to demonstrate their learning. Consider the evidence following the criteria as examples of artifacts you or other team members can provide or share with each other as well as other teams in your PLC. Note it is possible to circle criteria from multiple categories.

Getting Started	Implementing	Sustaining
Criteria: I sometimes, but not always, provide students with an opportunity to complete assessment opportunities after the final regularly scheduled whole-group assessment. I do not yet have a plan in place that allows all students multiple opportunities to demonstrate their understanding of classroom standards in various ways. Teacher-initiated spiraling is currently the only form of reassessment I use in my classroom. I do not reteach in small groups, differentiate instruction, or provide an alternate way of learning before a student reassesses.	**Criteria:** I provide individual students with additional opportunities to demonstrate understanding after the final regularly scheduled whole-group assessment. The additional opportunities may be based on the entire assessment or on specific standards. I have a plan in place that allows all students multiple opportunities to demonstrate their understanding of classroom standards in various ways; however, I am not sure if it is sustainable over time. Reassessment opportunities are either only teacher initiated or only student initiated.	**Criteria:** I provide individual students with additional opportunities to demonstrate understanding after the final regularly scheduled whole-group assessment. The additional opportunities are based on specific standards. I have a plan in place that allows all students multiple opportunities to demonstrate their understanding of classroom standards in various ways, and I regularly review this plan to ensure it is sustainable over time. Reassessment opportunities are both teacher and student initiated. For example, students are allowed to initiate reassessment opportunities on any assessment that was looped (teacher initiated) during the term.

Getting Started	Implementing	Sustaining
	I sometimes reteach in small groups, differentiate instruction, or provide an alternate way of learning before a student reassesses. I have communicated information related to reteaching and reassessment to parents, such as via a course syllabus.	I have built time into my class instruction to reteach in small groups, differentiate instruction, and provide an alternate way of learning before a student reassesses. I have communicated information related to reteaching and reassessment to parents in multiple ways, such as via a course syllabus and course website.
Evidence: Reassessment opportunities are not yet present. I have not yet documented a teacher reassessment plan. Reteaching or small-group instruction is not evident in lesson plans.	**Evidence:** Some, but not all, student assessments are targeted to specific standards. I lack comfort with my teacher reassessment plan, and it includes only either teacher- or student-initiated opportunities. Reteaching or small-group instruction is evident in lesson plans.	**Evidence:** Student reassessments are targeted to specific standards. I am very comfortable with my teacher reassessment plan, which includes teacher- and student-initiated opportunities. Students complete a learning (insurance) plan before reassessment opportunities. Reteaching or small-group instruction is evident in lesson plans and observable during daily instruction.

Continuum for Standards-Based Grading
Principle 1—Team Assessment

Directions: As a team, circle each criterion that aligns with your team's current level of implementation of the first standards-based grading principle—grades should communicate students' current levels of learning based on standards. Consider the evidence following the criteria as examples of artifacts your team members can provide or share with each other as well as other teams in your PLC. Note it is possible to circle criteria from multiple categories.

Getting Started	Implementing	Sustaining
Criteria: Our team has not yet identified priority standards for our courses or content areas.	**Criteria:** Our team has identified priority standards for some, but not all, of our courses or content areas.	**Criteria:** Our team has identified priority standards for all our courses or content areas. Each year, our team meets to consider revising the priority standards for our courses or content areas.
Evidence: The standards taught in a course or content area are dependent on individual teachers.	**Evidence:** Our team has a list of identified priority standards for one or several courses or content areas.	**Evidence:** Our team has a list of identified priority standards for each course or content area. Previous versions of priority standards and team minutes note the revision process used to review priority standards.

Continuum for Standards-Based Grading Principle 2—Team Assessment

Directions: As a team, circle each criterion that aligns with your team's current level of implementation of the second standards-based grading principle—homework should serve as ungraded practice. Consider the evidence following the criteria as examples of artifacts your team members can provide or share with each other as well as other teams in your PLC. Note it is possible to circle criteria from multiple categories.

Getting Started	Implementing	Sustaining
Criteria: Teachers on our team have not created a homework purpose statement.	**Criteria:** Some, but not all, of the teachers on our team have created a homework purpose statement.	**Criteria:** Our team has a unified homework purpose statement based on two homework questions.
Evidence: No homework purpose statements exist.	**Evidence:** Individual homework purpose statements on the team differ significantly from one another.	**Evidence:** The team has a single team-developed homework purpose statement that communicates the purpose of homework as practice, the ways the team is committed to differentiating homework tasks, and how the team will respond when students do not regularly complete their practice assignments, and it identifies students needing intervention.

Continuum for Standards-Based Grading
Principle 3—Team Assessment

Directions: As a team, circle each criterion that aligns with your team's current level of implementation of the third standards-based grading principle—students should have multiple opportunities to demonstrate their learning. Consider the evidence following the criteria as examples of artifacts your team members can provide or share with each other as well as other teams in your PLC. Note it is possible to circle criteria from multiple categories.

Getting Started	Implementing	Sustaining
Criteria: Teachers on our team have not created reassessment policies.	**Criteria:** Some, but not all, of the teachers on our team have created a reassessment policy.	**Criteria:** Our team has a unified reassessment policy based on the three important questions.
Evidence: No reassessment policies exist.	**Evidence:** Reassessment policies exist, but individual reassessment policies on the team differ significantly from one another.	**Evidence:** The single team-developed reassessment policy communicates the criteria students must meet to demonstrate readiness for a reassessment, when the students receive reassessment opportunities, and the parameters necessary to promote student and teacher time management.

Continuum for Implementing Standards-Based Grading Schoolwide or Districtwide

Directions: As a team, circle each criterion that aligns with your team's current level of implementation of standards-based grading across the building. Consider the evidence following the criteria as examples of artifacts your team can provide or share with school or district leaders or administration. Note it is possible to circle some of the criteria in the implementing category while circling some of the criteria in the sustaining category.

Getting Started	Implementing	Sustaining
Criteria: The building has not yet developed a common purpose of grading.	**Criteria:** Grading guidelines have been established at the team level, but not schoolwide, in order to communicate the purpose of grading.	**Criteria:** The building leadership team has established schoolwide grading guidelines. A schoolwide process is in place to determine letter grades from standards.
Evidence: No grading purpose statements exist. Grading policies and procedures are individually developed by teachers. No standards-based grading professional learning plan has been developed. The building leadership team has not discussed or considered changes to the master schedule supporting standards-based grading in a professional learning community.	**Evidence:** A team-developed grading purpose statement or grading guidelines exist. The building leadership team has developed a standards-based grading professional learning plan for the next semester or academic year and shared it with staff. The building leadership team has developed a master schedule change for the upcoming academic year.	**Evidence:** The building leadership team has agreed on buildingwide grading guidelines and shared them with key stakeholders. The building leadership team has developed a multiyear standards-based grading professional learning plan and shared it with key stakeholders inside and outside the school. The leadership team has tried out, evaluated, and revised a master schedule change to support remediation and enrichment opportunities for students.

Getting Started	Implementing	Sustaining
The leadership team has not discussed or considered possible standards-based grading implementation roadblocks. No leadership team agenda items or minutes document anticipated roadblocks.	The leadership team has shared the updated master schedule for the next academic year with staff. The leadership team has discussed a few, but not all, possible standards-based grading implementation roadblocks. Notes from leadership team minutes document a few possible roadblocks.	Leadership team minutes document discussion of the initial master schedule change and needed revisions. The leadership team has shared the revised master schedule with staff. The leadership team has extensively discussed possible standards-based grading implementation roadblocks and proactively communicated solutions with key stakeholders. The leadership team has shared a FAQ document with teachers and parents.

Action-Plan Template for Standards-Based Grading Principle 1

My current level on the continuum for the first standards-based grading principle—grades should communicate students' current levels of learning based on standards—is best described as (circle one):

Getting started   **Implementing**   **Sustaining**

Evidence I can provide to support my current level includes:

My next steps will be:

My team's current level on the continuum for the first standards-based grading principle—grades should communicate students' current levels of learning based on standards—is best described as (circle one):

Getting started   **Implementing**   **Sustaining**

Evidence my team can provide to support our current level includes:

page 1 of 2

Directions: Use the following table to plan your team's next steps.

Desired Level and Criteria: Where do we want to be?	Action: What do we need to do to move closer to sustaining on the standards-based grading continuum for this principle?	Change: What do we need to change or give up?	Evidence of Success: What products, policies, or procedures would demonstrate our desired criteria?

Action-Plan Template for Standards-Based Grading Principle 2

My current level on the continuum for the second standards-based grading principle—homework should serve as ungraded practice—is best described as (circle one):

Getting started   **Implementing**   **Sustaining**

Evidence I can provide to support my current level includes:

My next steps will be:

My team's current level on the continuum for the second standards-based grading principle—homework should serve as ungraded practice—is best described as (circle one):

Getting started   **Implementing**   **Sustaining**

Evidence my team can provide to support our current level includes:

page 1 of 2

Directions: Use the following table to plan your team's next steps.

Desired Level and Criteria: Where do we want to be?	Action: What do we need to do to move closer to sustaining on the standards-based grading continuum for this principle?	Change: What do we need to change or give up?	Evidence of Success: What products, policies, or procedures would demonstrate our desired criteria?

Action-Plan Template for Standards-Based Grading Principle 3

My current level on the continuum for the third standards-based grading principle—students should have multiple opportunities to demonstrate their learning—is best described as (circle one):

Getting started   **Implementing**   **Sustaining**

Evidence I can provide to support my current level includes:

My next steps will be:

My team's current level on the continuum for the third standards-based grading principle—students should have multiple opportunities to demonstrate their learning—is best described as (circle one):

Getting started   **Implementing**   **Sustaining**

Evidence my team can provide to support our current level includes:

page 1 of 2

Directions: Use the following table to plan your team's next steps.

Desired Level and Criteria: Where do we want to be?	Action: What do we need to do to move closer to sustaining on the standards-based grading continuum for this principle?	Change: What do we need to change or give up?	Evidence of Success: What products, policies, or procedures would demonstrate our desired criteria?

Action-Plan Template for Implementation of Standards-Based Grading Schoolwide or Districtwide

My team's current level on the continuum for implementing standards-based grading in a school or district is best described as (circle one):

Getting started   **Implementing**   **Sustaining**

Evidence my team can provide to support my current level includes:

Directions: Use the following table to plan your team's next steps.

Desired Level and Criteria: Where do we want to be?	Action: What do we need to do to move closer to sustaining on the standards-based grading continuum for schoolwide or districtwide implementation?	Change: What do we need to change or give up?	Evidence of Success: What products, policies, or procedures would demonstrate our desired criteria?

Other Resources

In this appendix, you will find a sample parent-communication letter, a series of sample schoolwide and districtwide standards-based grading guidelines, and a sample FAQ to use to help parents and other community stakeholders learn about standards-based grading practices and why they are effective.

Sample Parent-Communication Letter

In this section, figure B.1 shows a sample parent-communication letter to inform parents about a school or district's change to standards-based grading.

Dear parent or guardian:

Traditionally, grading in an English language arts classroom (or any classroom for that matter) centers on products (homework, projects, essays, and tests). A screenshot of a gradebook might look something like the following.

English Language Arts		
Date	**Assignment or Task**	**Score**
9/15	Test 1	20/20
9/20	Worksheet 1	5/5
9/25	Rough draft of essay	10/10
10/15	Second draft of essay	17/20
10/20	Worksheet 2	5/5
10/30	Final draft of essay	12/20

Figure B.1: Sample parent-communication letter.
continued ▶

Traditional grading creates a quandary in which points are simultaneously assigned for completing tasks (such as worksheet 1) and for demonstrating understanding of the big ideas in the course (such as the final draft of an essay). This is why we're using a different grading system in our class this year. Because we believe grades should solely communicate how much your child has learned in class, we will be using a system called standards-based grading.

The following is a screenshot of what a standards-based gradebook looks like.

English Language Arts		
Date	**Standard**	**Score**
9/15	Identify the theme or central idea of a text.	4
10/1	Cite evidence to support analysis.	3
10/14	Write arguments to support analysis.	4
10/30	Analyze the author's claims.	2
10/30	Determine the author's point of view.	1
	Key: 0 = No evidence of learning 1 = Minimal understanding 2 = Partial understanding 3 = Proficiency with standards 4 = Mastery of standards	

As you can see, in this version, learning is the primary area of focus. Each standard taught in the class (based on what the state says students should be learning) is assessed on a sliding five-level scale.

The standard scores will be entered at the end of each chapter or unit assessment. Students will also be given detailed feedback throughout the chapter or unit via ongoing formative assessment opportunities (such as quizzes and practice problems).

Students will have the opportunity to retake any assessment (test) before the end of the quarter to demonstrate their knowledge of the standards. An improved score replaces the old score in the gradebook so that they are not penalized for mastering a standard later than someone else. Retakes are only available to students who make arrangements one day ahead of time, and students may only schedule a retake after it is evident that new learning has taken place through extra help sessions, additional practice problems, or both, as determined by the teacher.

Standards-based grading gives students increased chances to learn, and it better communicates this learning with their parents via electronic gradebooks. We successfully piloted this style of reporting during the second semester of the 2018–2019 school year, and we will use it in your student's classroom this semester.

If you have any questions or concerns about standards-based grading, please do not hesitate to contact me.

Sample Schoolwide and Districtwide Standards-Based Grading Guidelines

In this section, we offer examples of standards-based grading guidelines used in the Solon Community School District and those of three other schools around the United States (used with permission). The following are the standards-based grading guidelines used in Solon Community School District (2012):

Purpose:

The primary purpose of grading in the Solon Community School District is to communicate achievement status to students, parents, and others.

Secondary purposes of grading include:

• providing feedback to students for self-assessment and growth

• encouraging student progress and self-monitoring of learning

Guidelines:

1. Entries in the gradebook that count toward the final grade will be limited to course or grade-level standards.
2. Extra credit will not be given at any time.
3. Students will be allowed multiple opportunities to demonstrate their understanding of classroom standards in various ways. Retakes and revisions will be allowed.

4. Teachers will determine gradebook entries by considering multiple points of data emphasizing the most recent data and provide evidence to support their determination.

5. Students will be provided multiple opportunities to practice standards independently through homework or other class work. Practice assignments and activities will be consistent with classroom standards for the purpose of providing feedback. Practice assignments, including homework, will not be included as part of the final grade.

The following are the standards-based grading guidelines used at Casco Bay High School (n.d.) in Portland, Maine:

1. Grades should clearly communicate what students know and are able to do in each class.

2. Students should have multiple opportunities to show what they know and can do.

3. Schools should support students in acquiring *all* of the essential knowledge and skills in a course, versus just a portion of it.

4. Academic knowledge and work habits are both important to acquire for college and life.

5. If students are working hard (as shown by their habits of work grade) to meet standards, they deserve more time and support to learn the material.

6. All students should have the opportunity to excel.

7. Regular communication with families about student progress supports deeper learning.

8. Learning cannot be averaged; students need time to practice and learn from mistakes.

The following are the standards-based grading guidelines used at Waukee Community School District (n.d.) in Waukee, Iowa:

Guiding Principles

1. Differentiation of instruction is necessary in order for students to grow and progress.

2. Behavior is not included in the proficiency indicator and will be reported separately.

3. Extra credit will not be given at any time.

4. Retakes and revisions will be allowed at teachers' discretion. Students will be allowed multiple opportunities to show mastery in various ways.

5. Teachers will determine proficiency by considering multiple points of data using the most recent data and provide evidence to support their determination.

6. Independent practice will be meaningful, purposeful, of high quality, and aligned with objectives. Students will have multiple opportunities for practice before the objectives are assessed for a proficiency score.

7. Students are expected to complete all assigned work. Teachers will allow students opportunities to complete work with no consequence to the proficiency indicator.

The following are the standards-based grading guidelines used at Bexley Middle School in Bexley, Ohio (Bexley City Schools, n.d.):

Grading and reporting belief system

We believe . . .

- The intended audiences for grade cards are students and their parents.
- The most accurate reporting systems are those that separate academic achievement from behavior reporting.
- Students deserve multiple opportunities to demonstrate what they know and can do after learning.
- Learning is a process and where you finish is more important than where you start or how long it took you to get there.

Sample Standards-Based Grading FAQ

The FAQs you use should help parents and other community stakeholders learn about your school or district's adoption of standards-based grading practices and why those practices will be effective. It will be important for the implementation team to keep a running list of questions that can be developed into a full FAQ for your district. The following text shows a sample FAQs excerpt you can use as the basis to create a similar resource for your school or district.

What is standards-based grading doing for students across the learning spectrum, including learners at risk and those identified as gifted?

Standards-based grading policies allow students multiple opportunities to succeed through reassessment. Students who may not learn concepts the first time they are presented are given opportunities to continue their learning and strive for mastery. Students who may struggle with traditional learning frameworks are often provided the opportunity to demonstrate their mastery of a concept in an innovative method during reassessment if necessary.

With traditional grading systems, work was due at a certain deadline, and failure to meet this deadline resulted in a zero or F. For students with work-avoidance tendencies, it is common to purposely miss the deadline in a traditional grading system so that they ultimately get out of doing the work and can pass part of the blame of their failure onto the grading system. With the flexible deadlines of standards-based grading, students are held accountable for completing the work even if they require additional time to do so. In a traditional grading system, the penalty for not doing the work is a 0, a penalty that research shows does little to motivate students who are at risk. With standards-based grading, the penalty for not doing the work is doing the work even if it takes longer than anticipated to complete.

Similarly, students who tend to catch on to concepts quickly are traditionally asked to complete the same homework assignments as their peers or risk losing points. In standards-based grading, homework is not assigned a point value; therefore, students who have a strong understanding of the standards to be practiced on the homework assignment may choose to not complete all the assignment and instead focus their time on other, more challenging, learning opportunities.

How do we motivate students to complete homework if it is not assigned a point value?

Parents and teachers can help motivate students by talking about the role of practice or homework. Because grading is meant to communicate learning, it is not a reward–punishment system. The ultimate goal is for students to demonstrate high levels of understanding by the end of a course. We also help students understand how the role of practice in sports or music is similar to that in learning. The reward is the game or performance. Student athletes are not rewarded after every practice. Having these conversations with students can help them rethink homework and understand it is an opportunity to make mistakes and receive feedback rather than merely accumulate points.

References and Resources

Aguilar, A. (2019, August 28). *Des Moines Public Schools shares experience with USD 259's new grading system*. Accessed at www.ksn.com/news/des-moines-public-schools-share-experience-with-usd-259s-new-grading-system on November 26, 2019.

Ainsworth, L. (2013). *Prioritizing the common core: Identifying specific standards to emphasize the most*. Englewood, CO: Houghton Mifflin Harcourt.

Ainsworth, L., & Viegut, D. (2006). *Common formative assessments: How to connect standards-based instruction and assessment*. Thousand Oaks, CA: Corwin Press.

AllThingsPLC. (n.d.). *PLC locator*. Accessed at www.allthingsplc.info/plc-locator/us on August 23, 2019.

Anderson, L. W., & Krathwohl, D. R. (Eds.). (2001). *A taxonomy for learning, teaching, and assessing: A revision of Bloom's taxonomy of educational objectives*. New York: Longman.

Bahrick, H. P., Bahrick, L. E., Bahrick, A. S., & Bahrick, P. E. (1993). Maintenance of foreign language vocabulary and the spacing effect. *Psychological Science*, *4*(5), 316–321.

Balch, D., Blanck, R., & Balch, D. H. (2016). Rubrics: Sharing the rules of the game. *Journal of Instructional Research*, *5*(1), 19–49.

Baş, G., Şenturk, C., & Ciğerci, F. M. (2017). Homework and academic achievement: A meta-analytic review of research. *Issues in Educational Research*, *27*(1), 31–50.

Bazemore, C. (2006). The "power" of a student information system. *Technical Horizons in Educaation Journal*, *33*(17). Accessed at https://thejournal.com/articles/2006/12/01/the-power-of-a-student-information-system.aspx?m=1 on August 22, 2019.

Bexley City Schools. (n.d.). *Standards-based grading*. Accessed at www.bexleyschools.org/sbg.aspx on December 6, 2019.

Board of Regents, State of Iowa. (n.d.). *Regent admission index*. Accessed at www.iowaregents.edu/institutions/higher-education-links/regent-admission-index on November 26, 2019.

Bramante, F., & Colby, R. (2012). *Off the clock: Moving education from time to competency*. Thousand Oaks, CA: Corwin Press.

Brookhart, S. M. (2008). *How to give effective feedback to your students*. Alexandria, VA: Association for Supervision and Curriculum Development.

Brookhart, S. M. (2011). Starting the conversation about grading. *Educational Leadership*, *69*(3), 10–14.

Buckmiller, T., & Peters, R. (2018). Getting a fair shot? *School Administrator*, *75*(2), 22–25.

Buffum, A., Mattos, M., & Malone, J. (2018). *Taking action: A handbook for RTI at Work™.* Bloomington, IN: Solution Tree Press.

Buffum, A., Mattos, M., & Weber, C. (2012). *Simplifying response to intervention: Four essential guiding principles.* Bloomington, IN: Solution Tree Press.

Campbell, C. (2012). Learning-centered grading practices. *Educational Leadership*, *41*(5), 30–33.

Casco Bay High School. (n.d.). *Casco Bay family grading guide.* Accessed at https://cbhs .portlandschools.org/UserFiles/Servers/Server_1098483/File/Migration/Casco-Bay-Family -Grading-Guide.pdf on December 6, 2019.

Conzemius, A. E., & O'Neill, J. (2014). *The handbook for SMART school teams: Revitalizing best practices for collaboration* (2nd ed.). Bloomington, IN: Solution Tree Press.

Cooper, H. (1989). *Homework.* White Plains, NY: Longman.

Crawford, J. (2011). *Using power standards to build an aligned curriculum: A process manual.* Thousand Oaks, CA: Corwin Press.

Dean, C. B., Hubbell, E. R., Pitler, H., & Stone, B. (2012). *Classroom instruction that works: Research-based strategies for increasing student achievement* (2nd ed.). Alexandria, VA: Association for Supervision and Curriculum Development.

Donohoo, J. (2017). *Collective efficacy: How educators' beliefs impact student learning.* Thousand Oaks, CA: Corwin Press.

DuFour, R. (2004). What is a professional learning community? *Educational Leadership*, *61*(8), 6–11.

DuFour, R. (2007). In praise of top-down leadership. *School Administrator*, *64*(10), 38–42.

DuFour, R., DuFour, R., & Eaker, R. (2008). *Revisiting Professional Learning Communities at Work: New insights for improving schools.* Bloomington, IN: Solution Tree Press.

DuFour, R., DuFour, R., Eaker, R., & Karhanek, G. (2010). *Raising the bar and closing the gap: Whatever it takes.* Bloomington, IN: Solution Tree Press.

DuFour, R., DuFour, R., Eaker, R., Many, T. W., & Mattos, M. (2016). *Learning by doing: A handbook for Professional Learning Communities at Work* (3rd ed.). Bloomington, IN: Solution Tree Press.

DuFour, R., & Marzano, R. J. (2011). *Leaders of learning: How district, school, and classroom leaders improve student achievement.* Bloomington, IN: Solution Tree Press.

Dweck, C. S. (2006). *Mindset: The new psychology of success.* New York: Random House.

Frankin, A., Buckmiller, T., & Kruse, J. (2016). Vocal and vehement: Understanding parents' aversion to standards-based grading. *International Journal of Social Science Studies*, *4*(11), 19–29.

Garry, A., Fodchuk, A., & Hobbs, L. (2018). *Personalizing learning through voice and choice.* Bloomington, IN: Solution Tree Press.

Graham, P., & Ferriter, W. M. (2010). *Building a Professional Learning Community at Work: A guide to the first year.* Bloomington, IN: Solution Tree Press.

Guskey, T. R. (2000). Grading policies that work against standards . . . and how to fix them. *NASSP Bulletin, 84*(620), 20–29.

Guskey, T. R. (2002). Computerized gradebooks and the myth of objectivity. *Phi Delta Kappan, 83*(10), 775–780.

Guskey, T. R. (2011). Five obstacles to grading reform. *Educational Leadership, 69*(3), 16–21.

Guskey, T. R. (2013). The case against percentage grades. *Educational Leadership, 71*(1), 68–72.

Guskey, T. R. (2015a). *On your mark: Challenging the conventions of grading and reporting.* Bloomington, IN: Solution Tree Press.

Guskey, T. R., (2015b). Mastery learning. In James D. Wright (Ed.), *International Encyclopedia of the Social and Behavioral Sciences* (2nd ed., Vol. 14, pp. 752–759). Oxford: Elsevier.

Guskey, T. R., & Jung, L. A. (2016). Grading: Why you should trust your judgment. *Educational Leadership, 73*(7), 50–54.

Hall, G. E., & Hord, S. M. (2015). *Implementing change: Patterns, principles, and potholes* (4th ed.). Boston: Pearson.

Hattie, J. (2009). *Visible learning: A synthesis of over 800 meta-analyses relating to achievement.* New York: Routledge.

Heflebower, T., Hoegh, J. K., & Warrick, P. B. (2014). *A school leader's guide to standards-based grading.* Bloomington, IN: Marzano Resources.

Heflebower, T., Hoegh, J. K., Warrick, P. B., & Flygare, J. (2019). *A teacher's guide to standards-based learning.* Bloomington, IN: Marzano Resources.

Hill, G. R. (2018). *Impact of teacher attitudes on implementation of a standards-based grading system.* Doctoral dissertation, Piedmont College, Demorest, Georgia. (ProQuest No. 13426348)

Hogan, P. (2011, March 30). Iowa schools to participate in federal anti-bullying survey. *Gazette.* Accessed at www.thegazette.com/2011/03/30/iowa-schools-to-participate-in-federal -anti-bullying-survey on November 18, 2019.

Holland, A. (2018, April 12). School board votes against standards-based grading. *Oskaloosa Herald.* Accessed at www.oskaloosa.com/news/local_news/school-board-votes -against-standards-based-grading/article_045740f7-5482-5f27-a3f4-59e8deeab6b3.html on July 17, 2019.

Iamarino, D. L. (2014). The benefits of standards-based grading: A critical evaluation of modern grading practices. *Current Issues in Education, 17*(2), 1–10.

Iowa Core. (n.d.). *K–12 Iowa Core in social studies.* Accessed at https://iowacore.gov/sites /default/files/k-12_socialstudies_508.pdf on November 19, 2019.

Jaschik, S. (2018, June 19). Chicago drops SAT/ACT requirement. Will others follow? *Inside Higher Ed.* Accessed at www.insidehighered.com/admissions/article/2018/06/19/university -chicago-drops-satact-requirement on August 23, 2019.

Johnston, P. (2018, November 22). Teachers "stressed" by new grading system. *Royal Gazette.* Accessed at www.royalgazette.com/education/article/20181122/teachers-stressed-by-new -grading-system on August 23, 2019.

Knight, M., & Cooper, R. (2019). Taking on a new grading system: The interconnected effects of standards-based grading on teaching, learning, assessment, and student behavior. *NASSP Bulletin, 103*(1), 65–92.

Marzano, R. J. (2010). *Formative assessment and standards-based grading*. Bloomington, IN: Marzano Resources.

Marzano, R. J., & Heflebower, T. (2011). Grades that show what students know. *Educational Leadership, 69*(3), 34–39.

Marzano, R. J., & Waters, T. (2009). *District leadership that works: Striking the right balance*. Bloomington, IN: Solution Tree Press.

McMillan, J. H. (2001). Secondary teachers' classroom assessment and grading practices. *Educational Measurement: Issues and Practice, 20*(1), 20–32.

McMillan, J. H., Myran, S., & Workman, D. (2002). Elementary teachers' classroom assessment and grading practices. *Journal of Educational Research, 95*(4), 203–213.

McTighe, J., & O'Connor, K. (2005). Seven practices for effective learning. *Educational Leadership, 63*(3), 10–17.

Moss, C. M., Brookhart, S. M., & Long, B. A. (2011). Knowing your learning target. *Educational Leadership, 68*(6), 66–69.

National Center on Safe Supportive Learning Environments. (n.d.). *Iowa*. Accessed at https://safesupportivelearning.ed.gov/state-profiles/iowa on December 2, 2019.

National Governors Association Center for Best Practices & Council of Chief State School Officers. (2010a). *Common Core State Standards for English language arts and literacy in history/social studies, science, and technical subjects*. Washington, DC: Authors. Accessed at www.corestandards.org/assets/CCSSI_ELA%20Standards.pdf on September 4, 2019.

National Governors Association Center for Best Practices & Council of Chief State School Officers. (2010b). *Common Core State Standards for mathematics*. Washington, DC: Authors. Accessed at www.corestandards.org/assets/CCSSI_Math%20Standards.pdf on September 4, 2019.

New England Secondary School Consortium. (n.d.). How do colleges view proficiency-based transcripts? *Leadership in Action*. Accessed at www.newenglandssc.org/wp-content/uploads/2017/03/NESSC_Briefing_NO16_College_Admissions_Know_More.pdf on August 23, 2019.

NGSS Lead States. (2013). *Next Generation Science Standards: For states, by states*. Washington, DC: National Academies Press.

O'Connor, K. (2007). *A repair kit for grading: Fifteen fixes for broken grades*. Portland, OR: Pearson Assessment Training Institute.

O'Connor, K. (2018). *How to grade for learning: Linking grades to standards* (4th ed.). Thousand Oaks, CA: Corwin Press.

Paulu, N. (1998). *Helping your students with homework: A guide for teachers*. Washington, DC: Office of Educational Research and Improvement, U.S. Department of Education. Accessed at https://www2.ed.gov/pubs/HelpingStudents/index.html on February 28, 2019.

Peters, R., & Buckmiller, T. (2014). Our grades were broken: Overcoming barriers and challenges to implementing standards-based grading. *Journal of Educational Leadership in Action, 2*(2). Accessed at www.lindenwood.edu/academics/beyond-the-classroom/publications/journal-of-educational-leadership-in-action/all-issues/previous-issues/volume-2-issue-2/our-grades-were-broken-overcoming-barriers-and-challenges-to-implementing-standards-based-grading on August 23, 2019.

Peters, R., Kruse, J., Buckmiller, T., & Townsley, M. (2017). "It's just not fair!" Making sense of secondary students' resistance to a standards-based grading initiative. *American Secondary Education, 45*(3), 9–28.

Pink, D. H. (2011). *Drive: The surprising truth about what motivates us.* New York: Riverhead Books.

Reeves, D. (2000). Standards are not enough: Essential transformations for school success. *NASSP Bulletin, 84*(620), 5–19.

Reeves, D. (2002). *The leader's guide to standards: A blueprint for educational equity and excellence.* San Francisco: Jossey-Bass.

Reeves, D. (2004). The case against the zero. *Phi Delta Kappan, 86*(4), 324–325.

Reeves, D. (2012, July). The ketchup solution. *American School Board Journal, 189*(7), 35–36.

Reeves, D. (2016). *FAST grading: A guide to implementing best practices.* Bloomington, IN: Solution Tree Press.

Roe, G. (2019, April 11). *A "better way to measure students' knowledge": Granite Schools using new grading scale.* Accessed at https://kutv.com/news/local/a-better-way-to-measure-students -knowledge-granite-schools-using-new-grading-scale on November 26, 2019.

Scherer, M. (2001). How and why standards can improve student achievement: A conversation with Robert J. Marzano. *Educational Leadership, 59*(1), 14–18.

Schiffman, M. P. (2016). *Standards-based grading: Educators' perceptions of the effects on teaching, student motivation, and assessment at the high school level.* Unpublished doctoral dissertation, Western Illinois University, Macomb.

Schimmer, T. (2016). *Grading from the inside out: Bringing accuracy to student assessment through a standards-based mindset.* Bloomington, IN: Solution Tree Press.

Schimmer, T., Hillman, G., & Stalets, M. (2018). *Standards-based learning in action: Moving from theory to practice.* Bloomington, IN: Solution Tree Press.

Shakespeare, W. (1935). *The tragedy of Romeo and Juliet.* New York: Heritage Press.

Solon Community School District. (2012). *Solon Community School District grading purpose and guidelines.* Accessed at https://sites.google.com/a/solon.k12.ia.us/standards-based -grading/purpose-guidelines on December 6, 2019.

Stallings, J. (1985). A study of implementation of Madeline Hunter's model and its effects on students. *Journal of Educational Research, 78*(6), 325–337.

Tomlinson, C. A., & Moon, T. R. (2013). *Assessment and student success in a differentiated classroom.* Alexandria, VA: Association for Supervision and Curriculum Development.

Townsley, M. (2018). Mastery-minded grading in secondary schools. *School Administrator, 75*(2), 16–21.

Townsley, M., Buckmiller, T., & Cooper, R. (2019, October 21). Anticipating a second wave of standards-based grading implementation and understanding the potential barriers: Perceptions of high school principals. *NASSP Bulletin, 103*(4), 281–299.

Urich, L. J. (2012). *Implementation of standards-based grading at the middle school level.* Unpublished doctoral dissertation, Iowa State University, Ames. Accessed at http://lib .dr.iastate.edu/etd/12492 on August 23, 2019.

Vatterott, C. (2010). Five hallmarks of good homework. *Educational Leadership, 68*(1), 10–15.

Vatterott, C. (2011). Making homework central to learning. *Educational Leadership, 69*(3), 60–64.

Vatterott, C. (2015). *Rethinking grading: Meaningful assessment for standards-based learning.* Alexandria, VA: Association for Supervision and Curriculum Development.

Vatterott, C. (2018). *Rethinking homework: Best practices that support diverse needs* (2nd ed.). Alexandria, VA: Association for Supervision and Curriculum Development.

Voelkel, R. H., & Chrispeels, J. H. (2017). Understanding the link between professional learning communities and teacher collective efficacy. *School Effectiveness and School Improvement, 28*(4), 505–526.

Waters, T., Marzano, R. J., & McNulty, B. (2003). *Balanced leadership: What 30 years of research tells us about the effect of leadership on student achievement.* Aurora, CO: McREL International.

Waukee Community School District. (n.d.). *Standards-based reporting.* Accessed at https://waukeeschools.org/academics/assessment/standards-based-reporting on December 6, 2019.

Webber Alder, C. (2019, March 27). Community pushes back against standards-based grading at Park City schools. *Park Record.* Accessed at www.parkrecord.com/news/community-pushes-back-against-standards-based-grading-at-park-city-schools on August 23, 2019.

Wiliam, D. (2016, April). The secret of effective feedback. *Educational Leadership, 73*(7), 10–15.

Winger, T. (2005). Grading to communicate. *Educational Leadership, 63*(3), 61–65.

Wormeli, R. (2011). Redos and retakes done right. *Educational Leadership, 69*(3), 22–26.

Index

Learning by Doing, Third Edition
Richard DuFour, Rebecca DuFour, Robert Eaker,
Thomas W. Many, and Mike Mattos
Discover how to transform your school or district
into a high-performing PLC. The third edition of this
comprehensive action guide offers new strategies for
addressing critical PLC topics, including hiring and
retaining new staff, creating team-developed common
formative assessments, and more.
BKF746

Proficiency-Based Grading in the Content Areas
Edited by Anthony R. Reibel and Eric Twadell
No matter the content area, evidence-based grading
puts student growth at the heart of the classroom.
Designed for teachers and administrators of grades
6–12, *Proficiency-Based Grading in the Content Areas*
details how to effectively implement evidence-based
grading and maintain its effectiveness over time.
BKF837

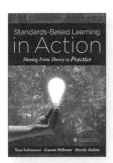

Standards-Based Learning in Action
Tom Schimmer, Garnet Hillman, and Mandy Stalets
Get past the knowing-doing gap and confidently
implement standards-based learning in your classroom,
school, or district. Each chapter offers readers a well-
thought-out action plan for implementation and effective
communication strategies for getting student and parent
buy-in.
BKF782

Get Set, Go
Thomas R. Guskey
A companion to the best-selling *On Your Mark*, this
practical guide details how to successfully lead lasting
grading reform. Dr. Thomas R. Guskey simplifies the
transition by guiding educators through six essential
steps—from developing a coalition devoted to change to
creating a systematic plan.
BKF929

Wait! Your professional development journey doesn't have to end with the last pages of this book.

We realize improving student learning doesn't happen overnight. And your school or district shouldn't be left to puzzle out all the details of this process alone.

No matter where you are on the journey, we're committed to helping you get to the next stage.

Take advantage of everything from **custom workshops** to **keynote presentations** and **interactive web and video conferencing**. We can even help you develop an action plan tailored to fit your specific needs.

Let's get the conversation started.

Call 888.763.9045 today.

SolutionTree.com